D1791602

Encore

The Leftovers Cookbook

Betty Jane Wylie

McClelland and Stewart

Copyright © 1979 by Betty Jane Wylie

ALL RIGHTS RESERVED

Reprinted in paperback 1982

The Canadian Publishers
McClelland and Stewart Limited
25 Hollinger Road
Toronto, Ontario M4B 3G2

Printed and bound in Canada
by John Deyell Company

Canadian Cataloguing in Publication Data

Wylie, Betty Jane, 1931 –
   Encore, the leftovers cookbook

Includes index.
ISBN 0-7710-9055-2

1. Cookery.   I. Title.

TX652.W95   641.5'52   C79-094467-7

Contents

Wylie's Table of Measurements

1 dollop equals 2 tablespoons
1 sloosh equals ½ cup
1 splash equals 1 teaspoon
1 dash, wet, equals ¾ teaspoon
1 dash, dry, equals ⅛ teaspoon
a sprinkle, as with cheese, equals ½ cup
to dot, as with butter, equals 1¼ to 2 tablespoons

Metric Conversion Table

The following charts and lists represent a guide only. There is no direct conversion for recipes, only some general rules and guidelines.

Metric Symbols to Remember

Quantity	Name of Unit	Symbol
Temperature	degree Celsius	°C
Volume	litre millilitre	 ml
Mass	gram kilogram	g kg
Length	metre centimetre	m cm
Energy	joule	J

Liquid Measure

A metric liquid measure cup contains 250 ml which is graduated in 25 ml divisions.

1 quart = 1.14 . 1 cup = approximately 285 ml.

Dry Measure

These measures are available in units of three: 250 ml, 125 ml, 50 ml. Conversion to metric usually involves a 5 per cent increase in amounts. All ingredients should be rounded up or down to the nearest unit. Small liquid and dry measures are available in sets of five: 1 ml, 2 ml, 5 ml, 15 ml, 25 ml. The 25 ml is similar to a typical coffee measure. All ingredients should be rounded to the nearest measure.

Mass (Weight)
You will need to know these units when shopping for meats, fruits, and vegetables.

1 kilogram (kg) = 1000 grams = a little more than 2 pounds.

Length
The centimetre (cm) slightly less than ½ inch is the common unit for measure.

Temperature — Celsius Scale
Freezing point of water 0°C = 32°F.
Boiling point of water 100°C = 212°F.

A Guide to new temperature:

250°F. = 121°C
300°F. = 149°C
325°F. = 160°C
350°F. = 175°C
375°F. = 190°C
425°F. = 220°C
450°F. = 230°C

Refrigerator Temperature = 4°C
Freezer Temperature = −18°C

For Liz, Kate, John, and Matt
who ate my failures

Introduction

My mother likes a chatty cookbook. So do I. A lot of cookbooks are so clinical they seem to divorce the foods they describe from human endeavour and taste. This one doesn't do that. I have always worked in a family kitchen, not in a domestic science laboratory. Every recipe in this book, every menu suggested, was family-tested, and I give you the honest reactions of my painfully frank children. It's hard to tell the truth, even about food, but I have tried.

This book is an honest frontal attack on leftovers. To launch or maintain this attack, one must have a sense of emergency. Consider yourself a vigilante committee of one, and keep a hawkeye on what goes into and comes out of your fridge, and when. The simple, but steadfast, rules of this vigilance are frugality, economy, and taste, which are all more important than ever in these days of rising prices.

There are a few things you should know. First, my test family had six members so, unless otherwise stated, all recipes will serve six. However, the ideas can be adapted to any size family. For a smaller family, storage may present a problem. It always does. Anything expands to fit the space allowed for it, unless it's rice, which always gets carried away.

Second, what I present to you is a philosophy of food, an approach – well, actually a way of life. The idea is to use the food before it becomes a potential penicillin culture in the back of your fridge. If you don't have a freezer to hide it in, or if the item has been sitting there taking up space for too long, give in. When in doubt, throw it out. But try not to let it get that far. Act before the mould sets in. Be in constant communication with the contents of your fridge, and keep the stock turning over.

Third, I got so tired of saying "pre-heated oven" that I stopped

9

saying it. I think there are only one or two recipes that call for a cold oven to start and then the call is loud and clear.

Fourth, the equipment required is fairly standard, except for the food processor which has recently arrived on the scene and has suddenly rendered half a dozen other small appliances obsolete. Certainly it makes leftovers a joy to create, though it is still being pushed as a high-class gourmet's friend. I still like to use some of my more traditional equipment, however, and I indicate what to use and when. The size of the food processor bowl tends to dictate what I use it for. The average one holds about three cups of liquid (there is a larger size on the market now) up to the top of the central shaft. In the case of lumpy, that is, less moist, mixtures, you can inch up that chimney because centrifugal (or is it centripetal?) force is going to keep the stuff plastered against the outside walls, like those motorcyclists you used to see in travelling circuses. Thus, the food processor will take a pound of peanuts for peanut butter, or up to half a pound of cut-up beef for steak tartare.

If I want to make one brioche loaf I use the f.p.; if I want to make bread I plunge in with my bare hands because what's the point of making bread at all if you don't make four to six loaves at a time? Similarly with cake batter: I prefer to use my mixer because I usually double my cake recipes, and the last thing I want is chocolate ooze down my drive shaft. The blender, too, still gets the nod for milkshakes, daiquiris, or a big pitcher of cold summer soup, but its tired motor is enjoying a semi-retirement because I don't force its attention on banana breads or liver pâté any more.

Either the blender or the food processor is useful to make baby food out of your one-serving dibs and dabs of leftover cooked vegetables and meats. The choice is yours, without salt.

I had finished writing this book when my husband suddenly died and changed the course of my life and the character of my kitchen. I felt I could not remove him from these pages, however. He is as much a part of them as I am. There is a joy in doing anything together, not the least being the daily, urgent, domestic struggle to keep a family fed, healthy, happy, and solvent. We did it together for twenty years. After all that time I bumped into him in the kitchen, even after he was gone.

Cherish the moments.

Chapter 1

Soup: A History

Hungry nostalgic writers seem to write at least one article a year recalling their grandmother's or their mother's kitchen redolent with the aroma of fresh-baked bread and soup gently simmering on the back of the stove (mine always simmers on the front burner because it's the biggest). The writers are usually men, and they usually conclude with gloomy satisfaction that you can hardly find fragrance, let alone food, like that any more. You can if you're serious about leftovers. Redolence is a concomitant grace bestowed on any household that produces its own soup. "Of soup and love," said Thomas Fuller, "the first is best." I love soup.

Soup companies have been boasting that the price of soup has changed little over the years in spite of the skyrocketing cost of living. Small wonder. I call my soups Something-for-Nothing Soups, because they're made out of what you would normally throw out. My children, less complimentary but terribly frank, call my soup Garbage Soup. At least, they used to. I've worked out a few alternate titles and managed to make them stick.

This chapter is about soup and all the leftovers that can find their way into the soup pot, with scant attention paid to what to do with leftover soup itself. What you do with soup is eat it (drink it?). Soup is never leftover; even if no one will touch it, you can cook something else in it. When all else fails, read this chapter again, and throw your leftovers into the stock pot. A great soup requires not a recipe, but a history.

Once you start making your own soup, you'll find that it rapidly gets ahead of you. Commercial canners of soup are very wise (not to mention canny) to put their soup in 10- or 20-ounce cans because it's guaranteed to be gone after one meal and then you have to buy more. I have an 8-quart soup pot and, take away the bones and other stuff, 6 quarts of soup goes a long way. No matter. Good soup makes good neighbours. Once you have accepted the soup pot as a permanent fixture of your stove, you will always have something to take to a neighbour suffering with a cold, a sick child, or a busy day. No wonder grandma was so good about sending soup to people in the olden days – she knew what I have discovered. You have to give some away if you want to preserve any pot or container in the house for any other purpose. And grandma didn't have a freezer, which I do. You know that joke about the man who went to the psychiatrist and said, "People think I'm crazy because I like pancakes," and the psychiatrist said, "That's nonsense, I like pancakes myself," and the man said, "Good, come to my place and see mine, I have three trunks full!" Well, you should see my freezer – it's full of soup.

It is also full of the makings of soup. There is an Italian proverb that says, "Old meat makes good soup." Remember it. Do not, under any circumstances, throw away a bone or a dab of vegetable for which you think you have no earthly use. Toss everything into a plastic bag and hurl it into the freezer. Pretty soon you'll have a bagful, or a lot of little bags full, of soup makings. Some of the best soups I have ever made evolved from discrete portions in the freezer. This is why I call my basic soup Evolution Soup.

Evolution Soup

Celery
Beef Bones
Water
Onion(s)
Salt
Bay leaves
Peppercorns
Carrots
Tomatoes
Lettuce leaves
Radishes
Green onions
Noodles or Barley or Rice
Kitchen Bouquet

Line the bottom of an 8-quart stock pot with the tops and leaves of the last bunch of celery you bought. Throw in the bones from a recent prime rib of roast beef or pot roast, and don't worry if they have been gnawed – the heat will sterilize them. Add the frozen bones from the last few steak dinners, or pork chop dinners, or whatever bones you had in the last month or so. Fill the pot two-thirds full with fresh cold water, or to cover the bones. If your bones are really terribly skimpy, you are allowed to buy a hunk of plate beef or a soup bone or some neck bones from your meat market. Put the pot on high heat while you roam around the kitchen for other ingredients. An onion or two, quartered, is always effective. Two tablespoons salt, 2 bay leaves, and 6 or 8 peppercorns will help. Scrape and slice and toss in 1 or 2 carrots. Now check your fridge for leftovers, because failing all else, you put everything that's left over into the soup pot. If there are things in your fridge you'd rather not talk about and that you hope everyone will have forgotten so they won't ask you where they are, toss them into the soup pot: soft tomatoes, coarse lettuce leaves, old radishes, tangled green onions, dibs and dabs of leftover cooked vegetables. The only exceptions I make are cauliflower, cabbage, and beets; all I find are too strong for this soup. I save the cauliflower for cream of cauliflower soup and the cabbage and beets for borscht. A few parsnips are fine, though. Stir down the liquid, which should have reached the boiling point by this time, skim the froth (if any), and cover the pot. Turn the heat down to simmer and forget about it for 3 or 4 hours. "To make a good soup the pot must only simmer or 'smile'" – so says a French proverb. My pot has a smile as enigmatic as the Mona Lisa's and twice as effective. You know it's there without looking.

When the stock has cooled, strain it and discard the bones and vegetables, then chill it well to congeal the fat for easy removal. If you're in a hurry to get rid of the fat, you can wrap a piece of cheesecloth around an ice cube and go fishing in the soup; a lot of fat does collect on the cloth in this way, but I prefer the longer, slower method of chilling for total fat removal. Now you can start adding deliberate fresh lumps. Egg noodles are nice, or alphabet noodles, or barley, or rice, cooked separately until tender and then added to the stock. You can finely chop fresh carrots and celery and add them along with any good bits of meat clinging to the soup bones. These vegetables will cook until just crispy-tender in your subsequent reheating process, or you can parboil them before you add them to the pot. Or you can buy packages of dried vegetables, which can be tossed in for fun. My son John looked in the soup pot just after I had added the contents of such a package and inquired, "Who put all the grass in the pot?" I'd hate to have had him overheard and misinterpreted.

Any interesting sauce (oh, but not hollandaise!) from your previous night's dinner might be added if you have no other plans for it, or, delightful bonus, broth from a boiled tongue. By now the liquid in your pot may with some justification be called soup. Start reheating, tasting, and adjusting the seasoning. I hesitate to be arbitrary here because one's taste buds are very personal. One of the most appalling soups I have ever tasted was given an unconditional guarantee by the co-author of the soup, the cook's husband. It took a great deal of doctoring, the one time I made it, to bring the soup around to our taste. As Guy de Maupassant said, "To be wanting in the sense of taste is to have a stupid mouth, just as one may have a stupid mind." Yet, as I say, taste is an arbitrary matter and quite subjective. And that horrible soup gave me one of my funniest lines. The base of it was a heart which had to be simmered for two days. The pot had almost welded to the stove. When I was dealing, finally, with the stock, my husband came along and said, "What are you doing?" And I said, "I'm straining my heart." It's not every day you get a chance to say a thing like that.

If your soup lacks colour — and sometimes it will — splash in a little Kitchen Bouquet. No dishwatery soup for me. As the days go by and you gradually diminish the soup, you will find there are appropriate liquids that will find their way into the pot: a drop or two of vegetable water, a few mushrooms left over from buying too many, the pan jelly from a mess of broiled chicken (chill the juices poured from the pan, lift off the fat, and drop the jelly into your soup — a rich addition), the liquid drained from a can of peas, or mushrooms, or what-have-you, a quarter cup of tomato juice from your husband's Bloody Marys. The possibilities are endless and the combinations limitless, with this exception: maintain your respect for food. Don't combine impossible ingredients and expect them to get along any better in the pot than they would in your stomach. Keep tasting; develop a sense for what will blend and what will not. Like every other aspect of leftover cooking, soup is a daily challenge. You simply must not let the smallest bit of edible food escape. It has a dollop of goodness to impart to the pot, maybe even a stray vitamin or a calorie of warmth to comfort one of the bodies in your care. My attitude toward soup exemplifies, in microcosm, my philosophy about all the food that passes through my kitchen: it must be loved, cherished, respected, handled with care, savoured with gusto, and *used up*.

A good soup pot is like Philomela's pitcher. Once it is operating it never seems to empty. Of course, you have to empty the pot once in a while to wash it and start again. And sometimes you hit a particular combination that your family tires of. Don't despair. Strain it (or not, depending on what's in it) and cook some rice in it. Call it risotto and serve it with pride and grated Parmesan cheese.

"A whole French family could live on what an English cook throws away," said Mrs. Ramsay in Virginia Woolf's *To the Lighthouse*. At no time are you more like that English cook than when you have company for dinner. I wonder sometimes whether my guests are all dieting or whether they really can't stand my cooking because the amount left on the plates when they come back to the kitchen is shocking: great shreds of salad left in the salad bowls,

14

crusts of garlic bread, bones with impolite gobbets of meat still on them, vegetables, and dabs of sauce. Now that's what I call the cost of high living. Don't throw anything away. Instead of scraping each plate into the garbage can, scrape it into the stock pot – everything, bread crusts and all – and cover it with water. Add an onion, salt, pepper, and bay leaf and leave it to simmer all night. (I'm assuming you started this soup pretty late at night, after your guests had gone, and you don't want to get up at four in the morning to turn it off.) The results are amazing. You get a distilled essence of the great dinner you served. (Have you ever tried Paella Soup?) The resulting stock will serve to moisten the genuine leftovers in the reheating process, or will serve as a base for a new Evolution Soup. Some of my greatest and probably unrepeatable – well, unduplicatable – soups have happened this way.

Nutritionists are always telling us not to throw away the water in which vegetables are cooked. We know about all those vitamins. But what about the vitamins we throw away without cooking? Potato peelings (scrub the potato first) may be added to the stock pot for extra taste, nourishment, and vitamin power.

With a blender or a food processor, no dab of leftover vegetable is going to go astray – cream of cauliflower, cream of broccoli, that's easy, but try this one.

November Pumpkin Soup

Begin by using a flashlight instead of a candle in your Hallowe'en pumpkin. Then you can have all that pumpkin as well as the gleam in your children's eyes. On November 1, cut up your pumpkin into 4- or 5-inch squares and put them in a roasting pan in about an inch of water. Bake them in a slow oven (300° F.) for an hour or so, until very tender. Remove from the oven and cool until you can handle the pieces. Then scrape the pumpkin flesh from the shell into the bowl of the food processor, fitted with the steel blade. You can push in about 2 cups at a time. In a matter of seconds you will have pumpkin mush, the stuff you buy canned when you're in a hurry and forgot to buy new flashlight batteries. You can pack this in freezer boxes in suitable amounts, and I'll tell you what to do with it all later. For now keep 1 cup of it for pumpkin soup.

In 2 tablespoons butter, sauté 1 large slice of onion until soft and yellow. Stir this into 2 cups chicken stock and heat. Into your

Pumpkin
Onion
Butter
Chicken stock
Milk
Flour
Light cream
Salt
Nutmeg
Dry sherry

15

f.p. bowl drop 1 cup cooked pumpkin mush, 1 cup milk, and 2 tablespoons flour. Blend with the steel blade, then stir into the hot chicken stock with 1 additional cup milk. Cook, stirring, and add enough light cream to thicken to desired consistency. Season with salt to taste, a grating of nutmeg, and ¼ cup dry sherry. Out of context like this, your Hallowe'en pumpkin will defy recognition.

If you love artichokes as we do, you will find that there are times you have in your enthusiasm cooked more than may be consumed at one meal. No matter. A leftover artichoke is cause for celebration. If you can snatch it away from someone who wants a light lunch of a cold artichoke with vinaigrette sauce, why not make soup?

Cream of Artichoke Soup

Artichokes
Milk
Flour
Chicken stock
Black pepper
Ground cloves
Dried parsley
Light cream
Dry sherry
Chives

Put the bottoms and lush scrapings of 3 cooked artichokes into the f.p. bowl with 1 cup milk and 2 tablespoons flour, and whirl up with one or three cycles of that determined steel blade. Stir this into 3 cups chicken stock, along with a grind of black pepper, a pinch of ground cloves, and 1 tablespoon dried parsley. Cook and stir until thickened and smooth. Strain; stir in ½ cup light cream and 2 tablespoons dry sherry and heat just enough to return to serving temperature – but do not boil. Serve with a sprinkle of fresh-snipped chives (or use the freeze-dried).

Chicken Stock

Well, I guess everyone knows how to make chicken stock. You get chicken stock when you stew a chicken. You can also get chicken stock by saving your chicken bones in bags in the freezer, the way you save your beef bones, until you have a stock pot full of them. In this case, you may throw in a package of necks and backs from the meat counter for extra meatiness, or save the giblets from your chickens along with the bones. Proceed as for Evolution Soup.

Ah, but there are many things you can do with chicken stock. French Onion Soup, for one thing, though most people prefer it with a beef base. And what about Garlic Soup? I think it's the closest thing there is to the legendary Stone Soup in the children's story. All you need is water and a stone – or a hunk of garlic.

16

Garlic Soup

Peel and slice the cloves from an entire bud of garlic and sauté them gently in 2 tablespoons salad oil until garlic is softened and yellow. Stir the garlic into 1½ quarts hot chicken stock, cover and simmer for half an hour. Strain the soup, heat to serving temperature, then add ¾ cup good dry sherry. Serve as you would French Onion Soup, under a slice of crusty French bread with a generous grating of Parmesan cheese and broiled just before taking it to the table. Serves six good friends enough garlic to ward off colds for some time.

Garlic
Salad oil
Chicken stock
Dry sherry
French bread
Parmesan cheese

Frequently, in the course of an adventurous cooking career, I have found myself forced by an unfeeling recipe to open a can of something in order to use 1 or 2 tablespoons of the contents. The recipe never gives a hint as to what you are supposed to do with the remainder of the can. Take tomato paste. You use 1 tablespoon of tomato paste in a pilaf or in the filling for dolmathes. The rest of the can has to be used up.

Tomato Tea

Dump whatever is left of your tomato paste and 2 tablespoons olive oil into a pot. Add 2 quarts hot chicken stock, 2 teaspoons sugar and ½ teaspoon crushed dried basil. Season to taste and re-heat to serving temperature.

Tomato paste
Olive oil
Chicken stock
Sugar
Basil

Every once in a while we have to cope with a coconut. My younger son received one in a basket of fruit when he broke his elbow. But once I had to cope with 18 coconuts because I had a birthday party with a Hawaiian theme for Liz and not one of her guests liked the coconut I bought for each of them; they left them all for me. When you operate on the premise, as I do, that it is a sin to throw anything out, those 18 coconuts presented quite a challenge. I learned more about coconuts than I cared to learn, as a matter of fact. For example, any baked good calling for coconut tastes about a million times better with freshly grated coconut than with the dried stuff. Dessicated, they call it, and I should think so. I also learned how to make coconut soup.

Coconut Soup

Milk
Fresh coconut
Chicken stock
Egg yolk

Well, it's not really coconut soup, but you can't make it without the coconut, so why not? And grating coconut with the aid of the whirling grating disc of the f.p. makes you feel smug and saves your aching fingers so much effort it's almost sinful. My 18 coconuts, however, were B.C. – Before Cuisinart. Pour 1½ cups scalded milk over 1 cup freshly grated coconut in a bowl and let it stand for an hour or so. Then strain the milk through a thin (old) dish towel, squeezing and mashing the coconut in the folds of the cloth to make it release the milk – which is now coconut-flavoured. That's all. Stir this milk gently into 3 cups hot chicken stock, blend in 1 egg yolk (carefully!), adjust the seasoning, heat, and serve. Best do this in a double boiler because the milk gives it a tendency to separate.

Remember the cook's definition of eternity? Two people and a ham. Eternity can be brought to a happy continuum if you make soup.

Stand-up Pea Soup

Ham bone
Water
Bay leaf
Peppercorns
Thyme
Onions
Celery leaves
Split peas

Put a ham bone, still generously fleshed, into the stock pot and fill the pot two-thirds full with water. Add 1 bay leaf, 10 peppercorns (live a little), ½ teaspoon thyme, and 2 medium onions, quartered, and any celery leaves you might have, if they're lying around not doing anything. Bring to a boil, skim if necessary, cover and simmer for 3 hours. Strain the stock, put it back in the pot with the shredded meat from the bones, and add 2 pounds dried green split peas and 2 medium onions, sliced. Boil gently over low heat (just above simmer) for 3 hours, stirring occasionally. Taste for salt now (seldom necessary) and adjust the seasoning.

This soup should be thick enough to stand a spoon in it. If it isn't and if you have some leftover vegetables in the fridge, say, some cooked green beans or wax beans or even peas, purée them in the blender or in the f.p. bowl with the steel blade, adding a little soup to guide them on their way, and stir this purée into the pea soup. More vitamins for the pot. If it's *too* thick on the second day, you may add a can of onion soup to thin it out. When you come to the end of this soup, you can make an easy bisque with the last of it.

18

Seafood Bisque

To the cup or so of leftover pea soup add a 10-ounce can tomato soup, 1 cup light cream, a 6-ounce can lobster or crabmeat, drained and flaked (cartilage removed), and ½ cup dry sherry. Heat in a double boiler over boiling water.

Pea soup
Tomato soup
Light cream
Lobster or Crabmeat
Dry sherry

What with the price of lobster and crabmeat (and everything else) these days, this is a lordly way of treating the last of the pea soup, I'll admit, and I don't do it very often. Instead I improvise. Perhaps there's a tiny bit of shrimp sauce from that easy sole recipe that everyone knows (sole, canned shrimp soup, splash of sherry, Parmesan cheese), and you couldn't bear to throw it out, of course. Stir it into the last of the pea soup. Maybe you had a rather thin cream sauce on a chicken à la king or something and when all the lumps had been eaten out of it, there's still some sauce left. Add that. You will end up with a delectable soup for two, if you're lucky—otherwise there'll be a fight over who gets it. Savour it because you'll never be able to duplicate it. But the next sequence will be just as good.

"Only the pure in heart can make a good soup," said Beethoven, and I guess he was right. Certainly you must have a pure tongue and impeccable taste buds. One hazard I should warn you about in making soup is in the tasting of it. Like every cook worth her salt, I'm a taster, and you must be, too. I taste and diddle and add things and taste some more until I judge the soup to be palatable, even appealing. But it turns out that I'm frequently too rash a taster. I don't seem to be able to wait until the soup in the spoon is cool enough to taste comfortably. The result is that I spend my winters (we'll talk about my summer soup soon) with the roof of my mouth scalded off. As fast as I grow some new epidermis up there I scald it with some more soup-testing. I'm sure I have the pinkest, youngest roof-of-mouth in the country because of it. You be careful.

Some of the greatest soups of the world are closely associated with the country of their origin. Scotch Broth is one of them, evocative of all the nice frugal methods of Scottish housewives. Leftover lamb makes a broth of a different colour so I've called it

Highland Broth

Lamb bone
Water
Celery
Onions
Carrots
Barley
Salt
Okra
Kitchen Bouquet

Treat your roast leg of lamb bone as you did your roast beef bones and start an Evolution Soup. Leave some flesh on the bone – you'll need it. Throw in all the lamb chop bones you've saved for the last few months. Plus celery, onions, carrots, the whole routine. Strain and cool the stock when the cooking time is finished. Save the bones. When the soup is cold, lift off and throw out all the congealed fat; drop in the shredded meat from the bones. (Now you can discard the bones.) Cook 1 cup barley in 3 cups salted boiling water until tender, about 1½ hours, adding more water if necessary. Drain the barley and add it to the lamb stock. Parboil 3 carrots (more if you like them), diced, and add them and their cooking water to the stock – there shouldn't be much. From there on, you're on your own. Add a 10-ounce package frozen okra (cooked and drained) if you like. Celery, too, not canned, of course. Lamb stock tends to look a little dishwatery so be sure to splash in some Kitchen Bouquet to make it look richer. Season to taste and simmer to blend the flavours and soften the celery before serving.

Years ago my Icelandic grandmother used to make a soup that she titled simply enough *bena supa* – bean soup. Served with a crusty homemade bread and a green salad, it is a meal in itself and one that you can be proud to serve to guests after a movie, a sleigh ride, or an evening at the theatre.

Bena Supa

White beans
Water
Salt
Onion
Stewing beef
Butter
Bay leaves
Beer
Mushrooms
Sour cream
Dill seed

Wash 2 pounds white beans and soak them overnight in enough cold water to cover them. In the morning add more water to cover, 1 tablespoon salt, and 1 large onion, quartered; boil gently until tender, about 1½ hours, depending on the beans. Beans vary. Test one every now and then. Skim the froth from the top of the pot frequently during the first half hour of cooking.

Quickly brown 3 pounds stewing beef, cut in small pieces, in 2 tablespoons butter, then add 2 bay leaves and 2 small onions, sliced; cover tightly and leave on low heat for an hour, or place in a 325° F. oven for an hour. I use a porcelain-covered cast-iron Dutch oven for this. Remove the bay leaves and add the cooked beans and bean liquor to the meat in the pot, stir gently to mix, and pour

20

in a 12-ounce bottle of beer, two if there doesn't seem to be enough liquid. In a separate pan, sauté 1 cup sliced small mushrooms in enough butter to lubricate the pan, just until the mushrooms are soft and golden. Quickly stir in 1 cup sour cream and 1 teaspoon dill seed that has been bruised in a mortar to release the flavour. Add the mushroom mixture to the soup, stir to blend, cover, and simmer the soup for 2 or 3 hours. Adjust the seasoning (this is when I burn the roof of my mouth). This soup is a beautiful colour and very thick. It will serve about 10 people, more if they aren't piggy about seconds, but don't count on it. If more liquid is required for another day's meal, simply add some beef stock or whatever you have lying around.

You will notice that the Bena Supa recipe, as it is written here, seems not to have been made from leftovers. Actually, it is all leftovers. Whenever I plan on a Fondue Bourguignonne, I buy 2 or 3 pounds of round steak when I buy the sirloin for the fondue. People don't generally eat all the meat we set out. Maybe they get tired of cooking it. Anyway, I add the cut-up round steak to the leftover uncooked sirloin steak and make a Beef Stroganoff, a generous one, generous enough that there are leftovers from that to make the Bena Supa, a great-tasting example of how one good thing leads to another. Add the cooked beans, the dill seed, and the beer to the leftover stroganoff, and you have Bena Supa. Of course, if you don't feel like going to all that trouble with the leftover raw fondue meat, make a Steak Tartare and be done with it. You can make Bena Supa from scratch next time if you want to.

I put my big soup pot in the garage (attached to the house) in the winter, to save steps when I retrieve it. In warmer months it goes in the overflow fridge in the basement. Don't worry about having a large amount of soup go sour on you. It never will if, each time you use it, you be sure to bring the soup to a boil. This, of course, assumes that you are serving soup almost daily. It's not going to sit there for weeks. If you can't use the soup within a week or ten days, give some away or freeze it. I must admit that the 8-quart stock pot has to find a place in the kitchen cupboard during the summer months. I continue to save all my bones, however. By fall I have a freezer full of bones, and seldom have to augment my soups from the meat counter until well after Christmas. But I still make soup in the summertime. A cold soup is a delightful beginning to a meal in the hot weather, and if you have unexpected guests as often as I do, you know that it serves the same purpose as soup in the winter—it helps fill the empty corners. You can also keep on using up your leftovers with your cold summer soups, although if you're in a real hurry, I'll allow you to open a can of something and blend it with buttermilk.

Buttermilk is the operative ingredient for an effective summer soup. Sour cream is good, too. Once I ruined a sour cream-based curry dip I was trying to make. It wouldn't go dippy; it insisted on staying soupy. So I gave it its head, threw in some leftover mushrooms and a can of cream of mushroom soup and oh, happy accident! Everyone was agog at my Cold Curried Mushroom Soup. (If you capitalize anything, it looks more believable, and has a ring of authority when you say it.) I often do it on purpose now, only sometimes I add dill weed instead of curry and then I call it Mushroom Dill Soup. If I were a home economist I'd probably call it Chilly Dilly Mushroom Soup, but even if I could stand to say it, my family would never let me get away with it.

You can go through the whole routine again, substituting crabmeat for the mushrooms. Or go back to buttermilk and make

Summer Tomato Soup

Tomato juice
Buttermilk
Basil

Pour equal parts of tomato juice and buttermilk in the blender and add ¼ teaspoon crushed dried basil. (I use this amount for a total of 4 cups of liquid.) Blend and serve. I do this only when I have buttermilk and tomato juice to get rid of, but it's good.

You'll note I refer to the blender now, and not the food processor. That's because I am a very sloshy cook and for me a little liquid goes a long way, usually down the front of my apron and all over the counter. The blender container holds more liquid than the f.p. container and gives me a fighting chance to get out of the kitchen dry.

Artichoke Soup (page 16) is very good served cold. Also the Pumpkin Soup (page 15). For that matter, almost any leftover cooked vegetables, such as cauliflower, asparagus, avocado, broccoli, peas, will grace the table again as a cold soup. In the case of a lumpy vegetable, I would prefer to use the relentless blade of a food processor to guarantee perfect smoothness in the end result, and you certainly don't want to dirty both machines, if you have them, so you have to make a choice.

Add buttermilk to any puréed vegetable, and an appropriate seasoning, blend, strain if necessary, and chill well before serving.

And don't forget vichysoisse – like a white velvet dream out of the food processor. Cold tongue broth, left to its own devices, will jelly and is delightful shivered as is into a bouillon cup with a wedge of lemon.

One has yet to consider what to do with leftover soup. Rice, of course, profits in taste and vitamin content if it is cooked in stock rather than water. So does a beef stew. An excellent sauce will result from the skilled alteration of some well-seasoned soup stock. The secret of French cooking, I have read, is never to cook anything in water; if you have enough soup around the house, you'll never have to.

Freeze soup in ice cube trays and when it is frozen, remove the soup cubes and store them in the freezer in plastic bags. These cubes then supply a fast hot mug of soup for a child's lunch or a bonus to an oven dish that requires additional liquid in the cooking process. Frozen in bowls to fit saucepans or in canister-squares, removed from the container when frozen and wrapped in foil for neat freezer-storage, blocks of soup make wonderful help-presents for neighbours with a crisis in the house.

Everyone should eat soup. The only one I know of who didn't was that poor nasty boy in Struwelpeter's horror poems for children who said: "Take the nasty soup away!" He died, of course.

Chapter 2

Meat: More Precious Than Gold

When I'm on a diet no one ever sees the roast beef again. Because I slice it and cut the fat off it and eat it for lunch. If, by preference and instinct, you like the beef better straight, then you are only reading this book for the fiction and not for the practical application of it. There are people who don't like leftovers dealt with any old how and my advice to them is: get born into a large family (and then try to get enough roast beef the first time around). My brother was one such unfortunate – a leftover-hater in a small family. He always used to ask where he was when the food was new. Answer: he was there all the time.

"Plain cooking," said the Countess Morphy, "should never be entrusted to plain cooks." The friend who gave me this recipe is a very beautiful woman. Trust her.

Cynthia's Caraway Beef

Butter
Onions
Mushrooms
Cooked beef
Beef stock
Flour
Salt
Caraway seeds
Sour cream
Rice or noodles or riced
 potatoes

Heat 4 tablespoons butter in a skillet – or, better, in a top-of-stove-to-oven-to-table casserole; sauté ¾ cup chopped onions in it till the onions are cowed. Add 2 cups sliced mushrooms and stir gently. Add 4 cups or so of cooked beef, cut in strips; cover and simmer for 10 minutes. You can be flexible about the amount of meat; why do you think there are so many mushrooms? Add 1 cup beef stock, stir, and cook over low heat another 10 minutes. Mix together 1½ tablespoons flour, 1 teaspoon salt, ½ teaspoon whole caraway seeds, crushed slightly in a mortar to release their flavour; stir the seasonings into 2 cups sour cream. Stir this into the meat mixture and cook till thick, but don't let it boil or the sour cream will do terrible things. If you're not serving this right away, with rice or noodles or riced potatoes, then reheat it in a double boiler so the sour cream will maintain its poise.

This next recipe is best cooked in a wok, if you have one.

Beef and Peppers

Seed and cut 1½ green peppers into long strips and sauté them in 3 tablespoons salad oil. With a garlic press, crush 4 cloves garlic over the peppers and add 2 or 3 cups cooked beef (which has been cut in long strips and dredged in a mixture of 3 tablespoons cornstarch, 3 tablespoons Japanese soy sauce, and not much salt and pepper to taste). Toss and sauté everything, then add 2 tomatoes, quartered, and ½ cup beef stock. Cook until the liquid thickens, stirring casually. Serve with crispy hot chow mein noodles. If you can get snow pea pods, and you can't always where I live, substitute 1½ cups of them for the green peppers, but add ¼ cup beef stock and cover and simmer them for 10 minutes before adding the beef strips.

Green peppers
Salad oil
Garlic
Cooked beef
Cornstarch
Japanese soy sauce
Salt and pepper
Tomatoes
Beef stock
Chow mein noodles
(Snow pea pods)

I guess everyone knows how to make Shepherd's Pie. With a food processor the hard grind is gone out of the preparation of the meat now, and the texture is incredible. Starting with the English accent of a Shepherd's Pie, make a tourtière.

Tourtière Anglaise

Get that happy steel blade busy chonking up your leftover roast beef with 2 onions, quartered (or else they'll hop around in an imitation of a sword dance), and 2 stale bread crusts and hope you have about 3 cups. If you have more you're in trouble because of the capacity of the food processor and you'll have to make 2 trips. Plop the mixture into a bowl and add a 10-ounce can of tomato sauce, or gravy, whichever comes to hand first, and the contents of an almost empty ketchup bottle (page 128), salt and pepper to taste, and mix well. Line a 9-inch pie pan with pastry, and spread the filling in the unbaked crust. Top with pastry, slash appropriately and bake 45 minutes in a 425° F. oven, or until the pastry is nicely browned. A nice variation: before you put on the top crust, sauté 1½ cups sliced mushrooms in 2 tablespoons butter till moist

Roast beef
Onions
Bread crusts
Tomato sauce or gravy
Ketchup
Salt and pepper
Pastry for 9-inch 2-crust
 pie
Mushrooms
Butter
Tarragon

+ mushroom
+ peas.

25

and warm but not oozy; spread over the meat filling. Season with a scant teaspoon of tarragon, crushed in your palm over the mushrooms, and then add the top crust. Proceed with the baking. This last is an especially good idea if the meat filling seems a little skimpy.

Or you can have hash in a bun.

Beef Rolls

Roast beef
Onions
Gravy
Ketchup
Salt and pepper
Flour
Baking powder
Salt
Salad oil
Milk

Drop chunks of leftover roast beef and 2 cut-up onions into the f.p. bowl for a few vicious cycles of the steel blade, to make 2 or 3 cups filling. If it looks as if there's room, add 1 cup gravy and the sloosh from a ketchup bottle (page 128), salt and pepper to taste, and allow them to be forcibly introduced. The goal is a mixture of spreading, as opposed to sloshy, consistency. Now make a quick biscuit dough: sift together 2 cups flour, 3 teaspoons baking powder, and 1 teaspoon salt. Add ⅓ cup salad oil and ⅔ cup milk all together, stir with a fork, knead five or six times on a floured board, and roll out to a rectangular shape. Spread the meat filling over the dough and roll it up lengthwise. Slice into 1½-inch thick slices and place, cut side down, in a greased 9-inch square pan. Bake 20 minutes in a 400° F. oven. Serve with extra gravy, or ketchup – a full bottle.

Roast beef bones are an asset no matter what their state: attached, detached, cooked, or raw. Detached, as from a prime rib roast you asked your butcher to bone and roll for spit roasting or barbecuing, the raw bones can go into a 325° F. oven for an hour or so with carrot sticks and par-boiled potatoes as their companions. The carrots and potatoes don't seem to know the difference between cooking with a roast or with its severed relations. Stir the vegetables once in a while to coat them in that lovely rendered beef fat, and salt them to taste before serving. You can even make gravy out of the pan drippings if you like.

Cooked bones, of course, go into your Evolution Soup (page 12), unless you deliberately leave so much flesh on them as to allow for broiled beef bones. This is an off-the-menu special at Sardi's in New York, but I had been doing it at home for years before I discovered that fact. Here a small family is a must, or else a many-ribbed roast.

Broiled Beef Bones

Allow one meaty cooked rib bone per person, or two if the person is large or the bones small. Dip each bone in a mixture of 2 eggs beaten with 2 tablespoons water and seasoned with salt and pepper and a dash of Worcestershire sauce; then dip in bread crumbs, being sure to coat the meat thoroughly. Broil the bones about 5 to 7 inches from the heat to allow the meat to get hot right through before the bread crumbs get too brown, about 10 minutes, turning. Serve with lots of paper napkins to allow handling and gnawing. If you're a sauce person, you might like a hot sauce with this; I like hot mustard.

Rib bones
Eggs
Water
Salt and pepper
Worcestershire sauce
Bread crumbs
(Hot mustard)

Then there's always a deep-dish beef and vegetable pie, which is as close as you can get to stew with roast beef.

Beef and Vegetable Pie

Peel 4 medium potatoes, then cut into bite-sized chunks; parboil them in salted water to cover. Drain, saving the water, and place the chunks in a greased casserole. Scrape 6 large carrots, then cut into bite-sized pieces; parboil them in the potato water and add them to the potatoes in the casserole. You can simmer small peeled onions in the same water or open a can of onions that you know are the right size, and add them, drained, to the vegetables. Add 3 cups cubed cooked beef to the vegetables and toss gently to mix everything up. Thin your leftover gravy with some of the vegetable water (pour the rest of the water into your stock pot) and check the seasoning, then stir the gravy into the meat and vegetables. Top with the following corn bread topping: mix ½ cup flour with ¾ cup cornmeal, 2 teaspoons baking powder, 1 teaspoon salt, and 1 tablespoon sugar. Combine 1 beaten egg with ½ cup milk and stir into the flour mixture. Add 2 tablespoons salad oil, stir to blend, and plop in spoonfuls over the meat mixture. Assuming the meat mixture is hot, bake for 20 to 25 minutes in a 400° F. oven. If it isn't hot, then put the casserole without the topping into the oven for 10 or 15 minutes until it is, then add the topping.

Potatoes
Carrots
Onions
Cooked beef
Gravy
Flour
Cornmeal
Baking powder
Salt
Sugar
Egg
Milk
Salad oil

Now let's get away from the potatoes and carrots and onions. Perhaps you think this next recipe should wait till I deal with macaroni, but leftovers are difficult to categorize. In this case, we're dealing with old roast beef; the macaroni is new.

27

Hot Beef and Macaroni Salad

Elbow macaroni
Cooked beef
Celery
Chives
Green onions
Red and green peppers
Tomato sauce
Horseradish

In a buttered casserole combine 2 cups cooked elbow macaroni, 2 or 3 cups cubed cooked beef, 1 cup chopped celery, 1 tablespoon snipped chives, 4 green onions, tops and bottoms, snipped (doesn't everyone use scissors to do this?), ½ cup each chopped red and green peppers, and 1 can (10-ounce size) tomato sauce mixed with 1 tablespoon horseradish, less if your children don't like things too hot. Toss well; adjust the seasoning and heat in a 350° F. oven for 45 minutes. This gets everything hot, but the vegetables are still crunchy because they haven't been precooked. Salad! Salud!

Almost all of the recipes I have discussed so far may be frozen, then eaten after they're forgotten, if you know what I mean. With the very definite exception of the last one; salads lose their crunchiness in the freezer. In dealing with leftovers, one cannot emphasize too much that *you* are not the victim. You're the one in charge. You blow the whistle. It pays to overestimate (I hesitate to say overcook for fear of being misunderstood) the amount of food you cook. Then you always have something to fall back on.

Of all the times when you need to fall back on something, the most common is right after you've had a baby. Most women fall back on their mothers. Failing that, fall back on your leftovers and, I hope, your freezer. Long ago, when we were still in the baby-making business, my husband and I, we really planned ahead and made our own TV dinners. I even used leftover TV dinner trays, saved for me by friends and relations. The very first menu was roast beef. And mixed vegetables and mashed potatoes. Easy to cook and to serve one Sunday before the baby was born, only we cooked huge quantities and served very little; then it was a matter of filling the dinner trays, adding gravy and butter where appropriate, wrapping and freezing. But not half as easy as later, when we drew out and heated our Wylie TV Dinners, as smug as if we had a maid in the kitchen.

Pork is a meat from which your leftovers decrease as your family increases. I suppose this is true of all meat, but there seems to be a standard-size pork roast beyond which they don't come any bigger. When we were two or three and one of us was small, there were more goodies left over than when there were six and all of us were large. Since you can't buy bigger pork roasts, the solution is to buy more of them, that is, if you want to make these good casseroles.

28

Pork Chop Suey

You start with leftover pork, cut up. With a little luck, you'll get about 3 cups from a cooked roast (or roasts). Take 1 green pepper, seeded and cut in nice little inch-long strips, 1 cup coarsely chopped celery, and 2 medium onions, also coarsely chopped; stir-fry in a couple of tablespoons of oil (preferably peanut oil here) for 3 or 4 minutes, or until everything is hot, but still good and crisp. Add the cut-up pork, 1 package (about 2 cups) fresh bean sprouts, rinsed and drained, ½ cup Japanese soy sauce and garlic salt to taste. Stir, cover and allow to simmer for no more than 10 minutes, just to be sure everything has a chance to shake hands and be warm and friendly but not sloppy. Serve with fluffy boiled rice. Have you noticed that cookbooks always say to serve this kind of thing with fluffy rice? Actually, I never have been able to produce really fluffy rice. Not what I call fluffy. Now, if you have leftover pork chop suey and leftover rice, fluff or no, combine the two into one gorgeous gloppy mixture, adding 1 or 2 cups beef stock to give it something to bathe in, and freeze it in a casserole or freezer container. I know the experts say you cannot freeze rice too successfully, but the extra stock seems to give the rice the life support it needs. Don't leave it in the freezer too long. Use it within a month, as indeed you'd be wise to use all cooked food like this. Then thaw it and reheat it in the oven for a leftover leftover meal. By that time no one will even remember whether or not your rice was once fluffy.

Cooked pork
Green pepper
Celery
Onions
Oil
Bean sprouts
Soy sauce
Garlic salt
Rice

Or you can compose a casserole of your own, starting with the basics of all casseroles.

Compose-a-Casserole – Pork

Sauté 1 cup chopped celery and 2 onions, chopped, in 2 or 3 tablespoons oil until vegetables are soft. Add 2 (or 3 or 4, depending on the size of your family and the pork roast) cups cut-up cooked pork, 1 teaspoon crushed dried thyme, and salt and pepper to taste. Stir, cover, and simmer over low heat for 15 minutes. Then you can add things: fresh mushrooms, sliced (try them added raw for a change, instead of cooking them with the onions and celery), and a can of mushroom soup. A cup or two of cooked macaroni if the pork is skimpy – or add it anyway, because it tastes good. A can of

Celery
Onions
Oil
Cooked pork
Thyme
Salt and pepper
Mushrooms
Mushroom or celery soup
Cooked macaroni or rice

celery soup instead of mushroom. Or try tomato soup, cooked rice instead of macaroni, and substitute green onions for the ordinary onions in the preamble, and add a little garlic. Heavenly to do this with cooked wild rice, should you ever have such an exotic leftover. A few leftover cooked red pepper strips or a spare cup of peas never hurt anyone in this context. You'll end up with a gorgeous casserole. Serve it with hot garlic bread and an enormous green salad and people will wish they had eaten less of the pork roast the first time around so that there would be even more of this.

Lamb is another meat that seems not quite so extendable as it was before our family grew up. Yet it's amazing how far a little lamb can go (all the way to school). Mind you, you have to be realistic about this sort of thing. I remember that I once made a beautiful casserole with some leftover lamb; it had *everything* in it, but not much lamb. One of the kids said, "I got a piece of meat!" and my husband and I both said at the same time, "You're lucky!" If you have more lamb than that, try stew.

Lamb and Dill

Onions
Celery
Butter
Flour
Milk and stock
White wine vinegar
Sugar
Egg yolk
Dill seed
Dill weed
Salt
Cooked lamb

I hate to be ubiquitous with the onions and celery, but there it is: start with 2 onions, chopped, and ¾ cup chopped celery, sautéed in 3 tablespoons butter until soft. Sprinkle 2 tablespoons flour over the vegetables and stir to blend it into the butter. Add 2 cups combined milk and stock (lamb broth would be nice) and stir to blend. Cook, stirring, until the sauce thickens, then stir in 1½ tablespoons white wine vinegar, 1 tablespoon sugar, and 1 egg yolk. Stir in 1 teaspoon dill seed, crushed in a mortar, ½ teaspoon dill weed, and salt to taste. Now stir in your cut-up lamb – at least 3 cups of it would be nice, more if you have it. You can serve this at once, as soon as the lamb is well and truly heated through, or you can turn the mixture into a casserole, refrigerate it, and heat it later in a 350° F. oven for an hour. I prefer make-ahead foods because they give you a chance to talk to your husband while dinner is in the oven.

Remember that line of Tennyson's, "I am a part of all that I have met"? It's true not only of what you have eaten, which shows (my experience always comes to the fore on my hips), but also in terms of the cooks you have known. There is something to be learned

30

from every cook and from every cookbook, if only in a negative sense. I had a very positive experience with a Swedish cook who came to tide me over the birth of one of our children (it was Matthew). She was inept with the kids but she was a wonder in the kitchen, and very jealous of her secrets. By the most fortuitous circumstances, I managed to one-up her and she opened her cookbooks and her head to me. Before she left us, I sat her down and said, "Now, about that corn pudding. Swedish pancakes. Cinnamon buns. Meat loaf." And on and on. The aforementioned fortuitous circumstances were that I was published in *Gourmet* magazine the month she was with us. Never before and never since – well, once, but then only in the letters to the editor, not paid, with a by-line. For the first time my Swedish friend felt she had met a peer with whom she could exchange confidences. She trusted that I would have a fellow-artist's appreciation for her techniques. And that's how I learned to put a cup of coffee with cream and sugar into my lamb gravy. Good gravy (see p. 121).

If you have a lot of leftover lamb you can always combine it with some cooked peas and a lot of that good gravy and put it in a deep dish with a pastry topping. That doesn't happen very often, though. Better to extend it with other things, throw in some curry, and pretend you meant to do this all along. The coffee gravy will have to adjust.

Lamb Curry

Surprise! This time cut up about 4 apples to sauté in 2 tablespoons butter, along with 2 onions, chopped. Add 2 tablespoons good Madras curry powder and cook-stir till apples and onions are soft and golden with curry. Add a handful (really, unless you have enormous hands) of raisins and 2 or 3 tablespoonfuls pine nuts, then stir in 2 or 3 or 3½ or 4 cups cut-up cooked lamb. Cover and simmer for 20 minutes to allow the curry to assert its dominion. Then stir in ½ to 1 cup of the lamb coffee gravy, heat some more (how long depends on how cold your gravy is), and serve immediately with cooked rice. Again, like the pork chop suey, leftover lamb curry can be combined with leftover cooked rice, and maybe a teeny bit more gravy or stock to keep that rice moist, and refrigerated for a later lunch – or even frozen for another meal a week or two later.

Apples
Butter
Onions
Curry powder
Raisins
Pine nuts
Cooked lamb
Lamb coffee gravy
Cooked rice

31

Everyone knows that Scotch broth is nothing without barley in it, but there is no such universal knowledge about the happy mating of lamb and barley in a casserole. What you're aiming for is a Scotch broth without the soup. Very nourishing. Would you call it Scotch stew?

New Lamb Pie

Cooked lamb	Cut up enough cooked roast lamb to make 3 or (better) 4 cups of meat. Now start with 2 onions, coarsely chopped and sautéed in 2 tablespoons butter or margarine until soft. Add the lamb, a 10-ounce package frozen okra, a 28-ounce can tomatoes, and salt to taste. Stir, gently breaking apart the okra, then cover and simmer this mixture for 20 minutes. You can do this ahead of time and refrigerate it in an oven-to-table dish until you start your dinner preparations. Then heat it in a 350° F. oven until the mixture is good and hot, about 20 to 30 minutes. Bring it out of the oven and turn the heat up to 425° F. Top the casserole with a biscuit topping rolled and cut to fit the top of the dish. Return to the oven and bake 20 to 25 minutes at 425° F. We served it with a raw zucchini salad which vegetable lovers appreciate and our children don't. The biscuit topping is the same recipe as in the Beef Rolls (see page 26). Serves eight.
Onions	
Butter	
Okra	
Tomatoes	
Salt	
Biscuit topping	

When I first got my food processor I chopped up everything in sight, including, almost, my own finger. One of the first things in sight was ham.

Ham Braid

Cooked ham	With the steel blade, zonk up enough leftover ham to produce 2 cups or so, adding ½ cup or enough mayonnaise to make it of sandwich-spreading consistency. Also drop in the feeding chimney 2 or 3 sticks of celery, 3 green onions, ¼ cup pickle relish or hot dog relish or a dill pickle – the f.p. is easy – and a tablespoon of wet, cool mustard (as opposed to the dry, hot kind). Now roll out the Homemade Biscuit Mix (page 82) into a rectangle and arrange this filling down the centre. Slash the dough on either side of the ham filling about one inch apart all the way down. Now bring these little tabs up and across the filling, alternating side, zik-zak, as you go. You see, it isn't *really* braided, it just looks that way. Tuck
Mayonnaise	
Celery	
Green onions	
Relish	
Mustard	
Biscuit dough	
Egg yolk	
Water	
Sesame seeds	

both ends around the filling neatly and lift the braid onto a cookie sheet with 2 spatulas. (It's all in the way you hold your tongue.) Brush it with 1 egg yolk beaten with 1 tablespoon water, then sprinkle sesame seeds over it, your generosity with the seeds depending on your affection for them. Bake the braid in a 375° F. oven for 30 minutes. Slice to serve.

Sandwich Filling

Then there is sandwich filling. With the f.p. and a little imagination you can do wonders with a cup or so of ground ham and anything else that's taking up space in the fridge. Pickle relish or corn relish, celery, green peppers, green onions, a sloosh from the last of a mustard jar, all these mix well with ham for a spicy sandwich filling. Or put a few ends of Cheddar cheese, or Gouda or Oka, or whatever ends of hard cheese you have, through the grinder or into the f.p. bowl (steel blade) with the last of the ham, spread it on a bun or toast, and broil it till that hidden cheese succumbs. Or for a sweet and sour taste, mix 1 cup ground ham with ½ cup brown sugar, 1 tablespoon cider vinegar, ¼ cup chopped or ground raisins (grind them in with the ham), or ¼ to ½ cup crushed drained pineapple; spread it on a pineapple slice and broil it. Better put a slice of buttered whole wheat toast under the pineapple slice or the filling will drop through the hole.

Cooked ham
Relish
Celery
Green peppers
Green onions
Mustard
Cheese
  or
Brown sugar
Cider Vinegar
Raisins
Pineapple

Easy Cassoulet

Start by having, on a few successive or closely related days, a ham or ham steaks, a small lamb roast with enough meat left on the bone to accommodate us, and a pork roast or pork tenderloin. It would be nice to have 1 cup of each kind of meat, cut into bite-sized chunks. The night before your Cassoulet, soak 1 cup washed navy beans in cold water and leave them overnight. In the morning add more water to cover the beans, 1 tablespoon salt, and 1 onion, quartered; bring the beans to a boil. Skim the water if it's foamy, then reduce the heat and boil gently until the beans are tender, maybe an hour – but test them for yourself. Remove from heat and allow to stand while you work. Sauté 2 onions, sliced, and 4 garlic cloves, sliced, in 2 tablespoons butter or margarine until soft and golden. Remove the garlic (if you can) and add 1 hot

Navy beans
Water
Salt
Onions
Garlic
Butter
Italian sausage
Thyme
Cooked ham, lamb, and
  pork

33

Italian sausage cut in 1-inch slices (about 12 chunks in all). Mash ¾ teaspoon thyme in the palm of your hand and sprinkle over the sausage and onions, then brown the sausage quickly. Now take a bean pot, preferably, or a good deep casserole and ladle some beans into the bottom. Dump in the ham chunks. Then another ladle of beans. Lamb chunks. Beans, pork chunks, beans, sausage and onions. Pour in enough pea soup (first choice), or stock or broth to cover the mixture, give it one good stir just to shake up the status quo, cover, and put the pot in a 300° F. oven for 3 hours. Check it occasionally, stir it, and add more broth or pea soup if necessary. Gorgeous. Serve it with homemade bread and a great big green salad. Leftovers fit for company.

There are two things made with leftover ham that most people forget about in the home and order only in restaurants. Both of them are more delectable at home because they're a) hotter, b) closer, and c) less expensive.

Reuben Sandwich

Sliced ham
Sauerkraut
Rye bread
Hot mustard
Swiss cheese

Which is sliced ham on heated sauerkraut on toasted rye bread spread with hot mustard, topped with Swiss cheese, and broiled. Nothing to it if you have leftover ham and sauerkraut. Strictly and traditionally speaking, a Reuben is made with corned beef, but I'm interdenominational when it comes to food.

And something else no self-respecting fridge should be without is leftover hollandaise sauce. Then you can have my favourite breakfast or brunch.

Eggs Benedict

English muffin
Butter
Ham
Poached egg
Hollandaise sauce

Which is a toasted English muffin, well buttered, topped with a warmed slice of ham, topped with a perfectly poached egg, topped with hot hollandaise sauce. Very simple. The trick is in the timing. You need to keep one eye on the toasting, one eye on the poaching, and both eyes on the Hollandaise. Leftover Hollandaise, by the way, can be revived with one more egg yolk and some gentle coaxing with a wire whisk (in a double boiler). It proves that leftovers can be sheer bliss.

34

Now we'll come back to earth.

Ham and Vegetable Pie

Cream ½ cup butter and add 6 egg yolks, ½ cup cottage cheese (a great way to use up the last of a carton of cottage cheese), and 2 tablespoons flour; beat, or put the whole mess into the blender or the f.p. (steel blade) and blend it if you don't like fine curds of cottage cheese floating around. Beat 6 egg whites until moist-stiff and fold in 1 tablespoon flour and 2 tablespoons grated Parmesan cheese. Gently fold the egg-white mixture into the egg-yolk mixture, then pour half of it into a buttered casserole. Mix 2 cups (about) cut-up cooked ham with 2 cups (maybe) vegetables and 2 tablespoons grated Parmesan cheese. (About the vegetables: almost anything goes – leftover cooked cauliflower is very good, also peas or green beans or mixed vegetables or broccoli. This is when you forestall the mould cultures on all the little dibs and dabs of vegetables you've stashed away in the fridge. You may not realize it, but you're destined to have one of the cleanest, neatest refrigerators on your block!) Spread the ham-vegetable mixture over the egg-glop and then sprinkle over that 1 can sliced mushrooms, drained, or a few chopped-up raw ones you might have lying around waiting to be remembered. Pour the remaining egg mixture over all this and then garnish the whole thing with 3 tablespoons grated Parmesan cheese. Put the casserole in a cold oven, closer to the bottom than to the top, and turn on the heat to 350° F. Bake for about 45 minutes or until the eggs have set. Put a clean table knife into it and if the eggs don't coat the knife, or stick to it, the casserole is ready to serve.

Butter
Eggs, separated
Cottage cheese
Flour
Parmesan cheese
Cooked ham
Cooked vegetables
Mushrooms

Well, I could go on and on about ham, but I don't want to be pedantic about it. There's always ham and macaroni moistened with a can of mushroom soup, and you can add a small can of oysters, either plain or smoked, just for fun and a taste sensation. Or make packaged macaroni and cheese and add the cut-up ham to that, plus some chopped celery and green pepper for crunch. Then there's scalloped potatoes – with nuggets of ham as well as onion slices between the layers of potatoes. The possibilities of a Compose-a-Casserole, using rice, are almost endless and slothfully easy if you use canned soup; ham and celery and rice and cream of celery soup (what about a little basil to liven it up?); ham and

mushrooms and rice and cream of chicken or mushroom soup –
spike this with tarragon. Or what about brown rice and ham and a
couple of tablespoons of parsley and a cup of pineapple tidbits,
drained, and a cream sauce with ¼ cup kirsch in it? Any or all of
these, once assembled, would bake 45 minutes in a 350° F. oven
and add up to an easy supper with the addition of a salad and hot
baking powder biscuits. I'm tired of talking about ham so I'm not
even going to mention stuffing peppers with a mixture of ham and
rice, or mixing ham with lima beans in either a tomato sauce or a
sour cream sauce. You're on your own.

People keep saying it's so charming to welcome your children into
the kitchen, that it's togetherness time and that's how they learn
to cook, and you don't want either sex to be helpless when it
comes to food preparation. Forget it. When I cook, I cook; when
they cook, they cook. I won't enquire into their methods and they
can do the same for me. There's a German proverb that goes: "He
who would not lose his appetite should not go into the kitchen."
    The first cookbook my first child ever received inspired both of
us. I said, "Go ahead," and went to have an afternoon nap. So
eight-year-old Liz made brownies and they were delicious. She
waited two or three months to tell me how she broke her first two
eggs – all over the floor. It was her problem, and she solved it.
Mind you, you should check the cookbooks your children use. My
son John decided to make cookies one day, and something, some
inner sense of disaster, prompted me to go to the kitchen in time to
see a soft appealing white mass festooned about my oven shelves.
"What are you doing melting marshmallows in the oven?" I asked,
seeking information only and trying to keep the sharp edge of
hysteria out of my voice. It turned out it wasn't marshmallows, it
was the plastic bowl with the batter in it. The cookbook merely
said to put the batter in the oven, so he did. Not a word about
putting it in a buttered 8″ × 8″ pan, nothing like that. Another
minute or so and it would have meant a new oven. Built-in, at
that.

Even the lowly wiener can be left over; it's not cooked, it's just
lonely. Make macaroni and cheese, maybe even a packaged effort,
and stir in penny slices of the wieners to make it a crafty wiener
lunch. Think about green onions, pimientos, sour cream in this
context, too, plus anything else your versatile fridge can offer. And
here's another possibility.

36

Wieners and Dumplings

Mix the contents of a 14-ounce can creamed corn with ½ cup milk, 2 tablespoons chopped onion, and salt and pepper to taste. Put the corn mixture into a buttered casserole and sprinkle over it 1-inch slices of wieners, cut from maybe 5 or 6 wieners if you have that many. Make a batter with 2 cups Homemade Biscuit Mix (page 82), ½ cup grated Cheddar cheese, and ¾ cup milk. Stir with a fork till blended and drop the batter by tablespoons around the perimeter of the casserole. Bake 35 minutes at 375° F. Serves four—a good thing when you're going out to dinner and leaving the kids at home.

Creamed corn
Milk
Onion
Salt and pepper
Wieners
Biscuit mix
Cheddar cheese

There are, of course, other casual things one can do with wieners. Cheese is a common companion, and onions. I have one friend who eats two or three wieners remaining in the package cold, standing up in her kitchen as she puts things away, and another who feeds the extras to her dachshund (this must be an analogy of sweets to the sweet); I don't consider either of these solutions fit for a cookbook about leftovers.

Liver is a meat you either like or don't; there doesn't seem to be any halfway feeling about it. On the whole, my family doesn't, so I try not to have liver left over. Hard enough to get them to eat it the first time around. However, there *are* times, and one must be ingenious. Actually, I had to be ingenious with liver from the time I was a bride, which doesn't seem fair. Turned out my husband was one of those who doesn't like liver. He made a deal with me: he would eat liver if I would cook it twelve different ways the first twelve times I served it. Deal. I learned a lot about liver that way.

Liver Pâté

Any time is the right time to make a liver pâté and there is practically no wrong way to make it, if you generally cook your liver as I do, that is, broil it until it is brown on the outside but still pink and juicy on the inside. Leftover liver like this will adapt very nicely to a pâté. Drop the liver in chewable chunks into the f.p. bowl with the steel blade in place, along with melted butter and a couple of tablespoons of brandy—say, 1 cup cut-up liver to 2 tablespoons butter and 2 of brandy. Add 1 teaspoon powdered mushrooms and a generous grind of black pepper. Usually the salt in the

Cooked liver
Butter
Brandy
Powdered mushrooms
Black pepper

butter is enough to salt this pâté, but use your own taste buds. Use an on-off technique with the steel blade and, for heaven's sake, check it after two on's or you may end up with something that looks like chocolate mousse. It's fun, sometimes, to add a few green onions to the mess; they adapt very quickly. Anything does, in a food processor. If you are still using a blender, take pity on that tired motor and put the brandy and butter in first, to give the blades a break.

Pack the liver pâté into a little crock and keep it refrigerated. It is excellent with crackers as an hors-d'oeuvre before dinner and it always seems to find an audience, even among non-liver-lovers. If the leftover liver has been skimpy, of course you can sauté a few fresh chicken livers in that butter and add it to the old stuff. The processor won't mind.

Did you ever notice that the only people in your family who don't like the food are the other people? It's not that women, who are usually the chief cooks in the house, like everything. The fact is that women are also the chief purchasers and they never buy anything they don't like. It's grossly unfair, of course, but it's one of the unsung perks of the job of chief cook. You like everything you cook and serve because you don't cook anything else. Unless you're incredibly selfless or on a diet.

Bacon is not a common leftover, but there are occasions when through lack of time or change of mind all the bacon cooked does not get eaten. Again, I certainly do *not* recommend nibbling it thoughtlessly as you clean up the kitchen. Delightful things can be done with bacon. Quite apart from bacon and peanut butter sandwiches on toast, or bacon and cheese or bacon and egg sandwiches, good salads, and sauces can thrive with the addition of some crumbled crisp bacon. As little as one leftover strip, crumbled, can enhance a quickie offering of Homemade Biscuit Mix Biscuits (see page 82). The delightful flavour of hashed brown potatoes (with onions) can do nothing but improve with a little crisp bacon added; ditto macaroni and cheese, or even spaghetti sauce. A tossed green salad, particularly one made with fresh tender spinach leaves, is gorgeous tossed with bacon bits. In fact, with the spinach salad, why not reheat the bacon fat and use it instead of the oil? Pour it hot over the greens and then add your vinegar and other seasonings plus the crumbled bacon. This particular taste combination is German in origin, I am told, and it really *schmecks*.

If you can't stand throwing out bacon fat, use it.

38

French Fried Potatoes

Peel 6 to 8 potatoes and cut them into strips that look as if they're going to be French fries, or use the f.p. ripple slicer if you have it. Soak them in a bowl of ice water for about an hour, then drain and dry them thoroughly between paper towels. Turn your oven on to 450° F.; melt ¾ cup bacon fat in a large shallow baking pan in the oven. When the fat is hot and sizzling, carefully add the potato strips to it. Toss them lightly so they are coated with fat, then shut the oven door and let them bake for half an hour, turning them 2 or 3 times. When they're crisp and golden, remove from the oven, lift the potatoes out of the pan, and drain on layers of paper towelling before you salt and serve them.

Potatoes
Ice water
Bacon fat
Salt

Lucius Beebe once called chicken the most important bird in the world. Who could disagree? I have one friend who serves chicken every time she has guests for dinner. The funny thing is that not only do her guests not notice that that's what they had last time, but she doesn't notice it either. She serves it so many different ways that you have to stop and think that after all what you had was chicken. There is no doubt that chicken is incredibly versatile.

The first time I cooked chicken I made $35. Well, not right away. But I wrote about my experience and sold the story for $35. It had to do with the fact that I could not put – was incapable, in fact, of putting – my hand into the insides of a chicken in order to pull out its innards. Few people have to face that problem today, what with assembly-line-grown-and-disembowelled chickens. After 20 years of facing facts in the kitchen, raw material no longer fills me with the dismay I can faintly remember feeling when I was a bride, but at the time my anguish was very real and my incapacity totally paralyzing. For several years after that first traumatic experience I bought cut-up chicken, preferring not to think about what went inside the bird. So it was quite a while before we ever had a roast chicken. Therefore, I was no help at all to another friend of mine who invited us for dinner one night and who underestimated the cooking time of her roast chicken. We all got hungrier and hungrier while we patiently waited for the drumstick to waggle freely within the skin. That is, we were patient; my friend's husband in his exasperated anxiety kept pouring us bigger and bigger before-dinner drinks while he made humorously barbed comments about the slow bird in the kitchen. Truth is, I don't remember much about that chicken when it was finally served.

You'd think with all this, I wouldn't know much about chicken, but I do. It's one of my favourite foods, new or old, and there are delectable ways of serving it as a leftover. My husband, for example, made the best club sandwiches in the whole world, and that is just the beginning of Chicken's Afterdays.

Bill's Club Sandwiches

The best way to write this recipe is in a column reading down the way the sandwich reads up:

1 slice toast, buttered and spread with
   horseradish (optional)
Sliced chicken, white meat
Dill pickle, thinly sliced
Crisp bacon
1 slice toast, buttered both sides, upper side spread
   with mustard (mild or hot, depending on taste)
Cheddar cheese, thinly sliced
Tomato, thinly sliced
Salt and ground black pepper
Lettuce
Butter and mayonnaise spread on
   1 slice toast

Cut in halves or quarters; anchor each section with a toothpick. If you want to be fancy, you can stick a stuffed olive on one or more of the toothpicks. *The Left-Handed Dictionary* describes a club sandwich as a sandwich that fights back. It's a great fight.

You can, of course, duplicate this sandwich with sliced white turkey meat. It is one of the joys of the twelve days of Christmas. Or Thanksgiving. A bird like turkey illustrates the real joy of leftover cooking: you never run out of something to do with it until it's all gone. Remember that old line about frugal people using every part of the goose but the honk? Well, with fowl you use every part of the chicken but the cluck, every part of the turkey but the gobble, every part of the goose but the honk, and I know a place where you can buy goose wing tips for feather dusters. Duck soup is very easy. So with fowl, slabs go into Mornay sauce, slices go into club sandwiches, bits go into pies and casseroles, grinds go into croquettes, the carcass goes into soup, and the cluck, gobble, and honk remain memories.

Nugget Casserole

Start after dinner on the night you have had a roast chicken (or turkey or goose). Dismember it as part of your clean-up operation and start your soup then, too, because the bones and gobbets from the plates can go into the soup pot as you're scraping and clearing. Spread out various sheets of plastic wrap and aluminum foil and have ready a large buttered casserole. If it was a large bird, you might have one breast intact; this can go as is into a double-folded wrap of plastic, then ditto of foil, then into a plastic bag and into the freezer. I take these precautions because most freezer instructions tell you you can't freeze cooked meat dry, that it has to be frozen in stock or gravy. I find you can, without loss of flavour or texture, if you use enough wrappings. Or you might want to slice the breast meat for club sandwiches. If I have to make a choice between the freezer or the sandwiches, I opt for the sandwiches. As you remove the stuffing, put it all into your large (2-quart) buttered casserole. Any leftover mashed potatoes and/or turnips can follow the stuffing. As you proceed to dismantle the bird, keep dropping meaty nuggets into this dish. Lots of ill-shaped but delightful morsels will meet no objections from their ultimate consumers. When the casserole is as full as you like, pour in the leftover gravy, preferably the kind with giblets in it. Make a few stabs at the mixture with a spoon to lubricate the stuffing and potatoes with the gravy and to mix in the meat. Allow to cool, if it hasn't already, then cover the dish with foil, label it, and freeze. Thawed later, much later – I have kept this in the freezer for 2 or 3 months – the casserole will bake at 350° F. for 1 hour. It may not look like much but it tastes beautiful. This casserole has been your by-product. Your prime object has been to fill sheets of plastic wrap and foil and freezer containers with slices and chunks and slabs of turkey or chicken. By the time you have wrapped everything, frozen it, refrigerated it, and put the bones into the soup pot, there is nothing left. Ever heard of a disappearing bird before?

And all those lovely chunks of meat in the fridge are ready to become almost anything you require of them. Ready?

Stuffing
Mashed potatoes or
 turnips
Cooked chicken
Gravy

Deep Dish Turkey Pie

Butter
Flour
Light cream
Turkey or chicken stock
Egg yolks
Parsley
Cooked turkey or
 chicken
Cooked mixed vegetables
Pimiento
Pastry topping

Or chicken. Make a cream sauce, using 2 tablespoons butter to 2 tablespoons flour and 1 cup light cream, and 1 cup turkey or chicken stock, depending on which meat you are using. After cooking and blending, stir a little of the hot sauce into the yolks of 2 eggs in a small bowl so as to introduce them gently, then stir this mixture into the sauce, along with 2 tablespoons dried parsley. Season to taste. Stir in 3 or 4 cups diced turkey (or chicken) meat – diced fairly large – and 2 cups cooked frozen mixed vegetables. If you have an open can of pimiento in the fridge, dice the little red jewel and drop that in the sauce too. (If you feel like opening a can just for me, did you know that you can freeze unused portions of pimiento? In a plastic freezer box.) Turn the mixture into a deep buttered casserole and top with a flaky pastry topping (see below). Bake in a 400° F. oven for 20 minutes. If you refrigerate this before baking, increase the baking time by 15 to 20 minutes, but watch that the pastry doesn't get too brown. If it threatens to do so, cover it with a piece of foil. If you notice any similarity between this recipe and the insides of a commercial frozen chicken or turkey pot pie, you're absolutely right, except this one has more meat in it. Instead of baking this in one big dish, I often divide the filling among 6 individual pie pans, the kind the commercial frozen stuff comes in, top them with pastry, unpricked, wrap them in foil, and freeze them. When you put them in the oven direct from the freezer, you must prick them and bake them as the frozen ones are baked: in a 425° F. oven for 40 minutes.

The pastry topping, by the way, is a lovely flaky one, equally suitable for dessert pies.

Pastry Topping for All Kinds of Meat Pies

Flour
Salt
Shortening
Ice water

Sift together 4 cups flour and 1⅓ teaspoons salt into a large bowl. Cut into it 2 cups vegetable shortening and blend with a pastry blender until the mixture resembles cornmeal. With a fork stir in 6 to 8 tablespoons ice water and then round up the pastry with your hands. Form into one large (huge!) or two smaller balls and chunk one on top of the other onto a large sheet of waxed paper. Tightly wrap the pastry, put it in a plastic bag, and into the fridge for at least an hour. Roll out on a floured board and cut to the desired shape. This is a large recipe and will make a goodly number of individual meat pies. Refrigerated, it will keep for 2 weeks. If it is very hard and cold when you remove it from the fridge, soften a working-size piece of it in your hands before you begin to roll it out.

You can do a chicken chop suey as you do Pork Chop Suey and serve it with fluffy boiled rice. But the Compose-a-Casserole idea holds as well with chicken and turkey. Just keep in mind all of your options.

Compose-a-Casserole for Chicken or Turkey

Melt 4 tablespoons butter or margarine and blend in 4 tablespoons flour. Add 2 cups milk gradually, stirring, and then 2 cups chicken or turkey stock. Stir and cook until the sauce is thickened, then stir in about a cup of grated or cut-up Cheddar cheese, or a combination of old bits of cheeses you may want to use up—nothing too sharp or strong though. Blend in the cheese as it melts and then season the sauce to taste with salt, pepper, Worcestershire sauce, maybe a splash (¼ cup) of sherry. Now stir in 4 cups or so cut-up chicken (or turkey) meat, 1 cup chopped celery, 1 green pepper, diced, maybe some mushrooms—1 can, drained, or 1 cup cut-up fresh ones—if you're short on meat. I like the crunchiness of the celery and green pepper in this casserole without the pre-softening in butter. This mixture can be turned into a casserole on top of 8 ounces wide egg noodles, cooked and drained, or on top of 3 cups cooked rice, whichever appeals to you (I go for the noodles). You can add cut-up pimientos or leftover cooked red peppers, or even a few leftover cooked peas (1 cup), if you have them. A hard-boiled egg could be sliced and arranged neatly on top of the casserole, then sprinkled with buttered bread crumbs and more grated Cheddar cheese, up to ½ cup. Or sprinkle crumbled crisp bacon on top of the egg slices. Or whatever. Bake 1 hour at 350° F.

At one time I wondered at anyone having the patience to butter bread crumbs when it's so much easier to strew dots of butter artistically over the arena of crumbled bread. My problem is I have too vivid an imagination. When dealing with food, this is not always an advantage. Pragmatism counts.

Butter
Flour
Milk
Chicken or turkey stock
Cheddar cheese
Salt and pepper
Worcestershire sauce
Sherry
Cooked chicken or
 turkey
Celery
Green pepper
Mushrooms
Egg noodles or rice

This one makes a nice luncheon for guests.

Turkey or Chicken Divan

Broccoli
White turkey or chicken
  meat
Butter
Flour
Half-and-half or light
  cream
Turkey or chicken stock
Worcestershire sauce
Sherry
Heavy cream
Parmesan cheese

Cook enough broccoli for six people – you know your people better than I do. In our family only the adults eat the flowerets; the children, under pressure, eat the stems. You can use fresh or frozen broccoli, but cook it until barely tender, drain it, and lay it neatly in a large flat buttered baking dish. Cover the broccoli with thick slices of white turkey or chicken meat and pour over it the following sauce. Melt 2 tablespoons butter or margarine and stir in 2 tablespoons flour; cook it for a moment or two. Stir in a total of 2 cups half-and-half or light cream, and turkey or chicken stock. Cook and stir the sauce until thickened, adjust the seasoning, and add a splash of Worcestershire sauce and ⅓ cup sherry. Stir in ½ cup heavy cream, whipped till thick but not stiff, and 1 cup grated Parmesan cheese. When you have poured the sauce over the meat, you might sprinkle a little more Parmesan cheese over the top so it will brown nicely in the oven. Bake 20 to 25 minutes at 350° F. if you do it right away; if refrigerated beforehand it will need 40 to 45 minutes. If you like, you can make this in individual shallow casserole dishes.

I have another dramatic way of serving turkey.

Turkey and Oysters

Butter
Flour
Light cream
Turkey stock
Salt and pepper
Worcestershire sauce
Sherry
Parsley
White turkey meat
Oysters
Parmesan cheese

Prepare your usual white sauce (2 tablespoons butter, 2 tablespoons flour, a total of 2 cups light cream and turkey stock) seasoned with salt and pepper, Worcestershire sauce, ¼ cup sherry, and 2 generous tablespoons snipped parsley. Blend and cook the sauce until it is very smooth and very hot. Now – in a flat buttered casserole – lay a bed of sliced white turkey meat, enough for 6 servings is the best way to put it, since you can't stuff slices into a cup to measure them. Scatter over the turkey 1 cup freshly shucked (or bulk) oysters. In the landlocked area where I live, it is easier to obtain oysters in bulk than it is to get them in the shell. Pour the hot sauce over the turkey and oysters; slide the casserole into a 350° F. oven for 15 minutes – long enough to get everything hot but not to damage the oysters. Then quickly sprinkle grated Parmesan cheese over the sauce and pop everything back under the broiler to brown. Serve immediately. If you don't like, or can't get, oysters, try fresh mushrooms, little button ones, uncooked.

I always used to wonder what "optional" meant in a recipe. I myself have used the word – in the recipe for club sandwiches. I described the horseradish as optional, in case you don't like it. But other times, optional means I don't like it, but you might. Or maybe it's merely the cook's way of saying she can't make up her mind whether she likes the recipe better with or without black olives. I think it best to keep an open mind about optional. You never know when it might come in handy since there's no accounting for tastes.

In his *Jug of Wine* cookbook Morrison Wood describes a lovely treat which carries with it a story. *La Médiatrice* was the French bread stuffed with oysters which southern gentlemen were supposed to have given their wives to pacify them when the men stayed out too late drinking. I adapted the idea to pacify guests at a late after-theatre supper.

Chicken in a Loaf

Slice a loaf of French bread into 6 very thick slices, trimming off the end crusts. Cut each slice in half horizontally and hollow out a little of the inside. Don't throw away the bread you hollow out! Use it for stuffing, meat loaf, a bread crumb topping for a casserole, but don't throw it away! Crush 6 cloves garlic into ⅔ cup soft butter or margarine. Add 1 scant teaspoon each dried parsley and poultry seasoning and mash it all together. Spread each horizontal slice of the bread generously with this butter. Now place 2 or 3 good-sized slices or 1 solid large slab of leftover cooked breast of chicken on the bottom slice of bread, and cover with the corresponding top slice. Wrap each sandwich individually in foil; warm in a 300°F. oven for half an hour – longer if cold from the refrigerator. And don't worry about it if your guests decide to have another drink before they eat. Serve hot. This is with leftovers, of course. If you really want to go all out with this, try it with an individual chicken breast, sautéed in butter until tender, as the filling for each garlic buttered sandwich. Then it becomes so substantial it's a dinner-size meal.

French bread
Garlic
Butter
Parsley
Poultry seasoning
Cooked breast of chicken

Somewhere deep in my subconscious there is an image of croquettes and that image is hard to shake. I think it stems from those hygienic booklets that were produced during the thirties, showing the modern housewife how to use her new electric stove. I have

45

inherited some of my mother's booklets and they seem to me to be so sterile and so pat that one cannot imagine anyone following their prissy instructions. Croquettes make me think of page three of the Dietitian's Handbook. Nevertheless, the croquette is a very useful and delicious way of producing a meal from very little meat and is the kind of thing the food processor loves to help with. In the beginning there was the bird, then there were slices and chunks, now you're down to hash and bits. "After all," said Irvin Cobb, "what is a croquette but hash that has come to a head?"

Chicken Croquettes

Butter
Flour
Cream
Ground chicken
Parsley
Chives
Salt and pepper
Egg
Water
Bread crumbs
Fat

Drop chunks and pieces of the last gobbets of chicken you can rip off the carcass into the understanding bowl of your f.p. with a couple of sprigs of parsley and some chives if you have a pot on your windowsill, and salt and pepper to taste, and you're lucky if it amounts to 3 cups, chopped. Make a thick cream sauce (2 tablespoons butter or margarine to 2 tablespoons flour, ½ cup cream), and add it to the mixture in the bowl, blending it in (steel blade for all this). Moisten your hands with cold water and shape a handful of this (thick) mixture into a long oval rectangle – in other words, into a croquette shape. Carry on this way until you have used up all the mixture and your hands are so yecchy you can't stand them. Then dip each croquette into an egg beaten with 1 tablespoon water, and then into dry seasoned bread crumbs (and guess who made the bread crumbs in what bowl of whose food processor?). Chill. Heat deep fat to 390° F. and fry the croquettes, as many at a time as will comfortably fit into the basket, for 5 minutes or until nicely browned on the outside. As you remove them from the fryer, put them on a warming pan covered with several thicknesses of paper towelling to drain the fat. Keep them warm in a 250° F. oven until all are done.

I guess everyone knows about tetrazzini. It's considered a great company dish, very good for buffet dinners because it's a recipe that is easily doubled, tripled, or quadrupled, can be made well in advance, and nobody dislikes it. Once you've made it a couple of times, it takes over and guides your hand. All sorts of goodies can find their way into a warm and welcoming tangle of spaghetti. It's a great way to use up leftover chicken for a family meal. Turkey, too, only then, of course, you call it Turkey Tetrazzini.

Chicken Tetrazzini

All right, another cream sauce. This time make it 4 tablespoons butter to 4 tablespoons flour, blended with 1½ cups milk and 1 cup white wine, salt and pepper to taste, and a generous grating (½ teaspoon) of nutmeg. Leave the sauce on simmer (or low) and in another pan sauté 2 onions, chopped, and ½ cup each chopped green and red pepper in 2 tablespoons butter. When these vegetables are suitably soft, add 1 cup sliced fresh mushrooms, and cook them gently and briefly. Now add at least 2 cups cooked chicken, cut in big chunks, lots more if you have it, up to 5 cups if you're lucky. Turn the heat off and ignore that pan for a while, too. This recipe dirties lots of utensils so it's a good thing to make it ahead of time. Boil 8 ounces vermicelli until *al dente* or really tender, whichever you prefer, drain and rinse it, and put it into a large, preferably shallow rather than deep, buttered casserole. Now combine the sauce with the chicken-veg. mixture and pour the whole mess over the vermicelli. Poke at it kind of artistically with your spoon to let the sauce seep into the pasta and to give all those good chunks of food a chance to look casual and inviting at the same time. Now you can refrigerate it, covered with foil or plastic wrap, and proceed to clean up your messy kitchen. Bring it out about half an hour before you cook it to give it a chance to come up to room temperature. Before you pop this gorgeous creation into a 375° F. oven, sprinkle over it 1 cup grated cheese – half Parmesan and half Cheddar. Bake 45 to 60 minutes.

Butter
Flour
Milk
White wine
Salt and pepper
Nutmeg
Onions
Green and red pepper
Mushrooms
Cooked Chicken
Vermicelli
Parmesan cheese
Cheddar cheese

The last little bits of chicken will make a good lunch if you combine them with an 8-ounce package of fine egg noodles boiled till tender, drained, and tossed with ½ cup soft butter or margarine. Add a little garlic salt when you season this.

Perhaps it was a good thing that I had such trouble with my first chicken. It taught me great respect for the bird.

Chapter 3

Fish in the Unruffled Lakes

Fish in the unruffled lakes have nothing to do with leftover fish in a harassed kitchen, but I like that phrase of W. H. Auden's. Our children are not generally very fond of fish; I tend to want to make a generalization out of this – that therefore all children do not like fish very much – but I know that does not necessarily follow. All I'm trying to say is that if you think it's hard to get them to eat fish the first time, just think what a challenge it is to get them to eat it the second time around. "One man's fish is another man's *poisson*." I was interested to discover that American writer Carolyn Wells is credited with having originated that line. She must have had kids who didn't like fish.

But it's a vicious circle. The fact that they don't like it the first time guarantees that there's fish left over to serve the second time because they don't eat it all the first time. You have to start with something they do like and sort of sneak the fish in with it.

Fish Fry

Onions
Butter
Cooked potatoes
Cooked fish
Salt
Black pepper

Slice 2 onions into 3 tablespoons butter or margarine in a frying pan and bring them along until they're golden. Add 1 cup or so diced cooked potatoes, the amount here depending on how much leftover potato you have. (It might be wise to plan on having some so you can use up the fish.) Stir and fry the potatoes and onions until they're browning nicely, then stir in 1 cup flaked cooked fish. Season to taste with salt and a generous grind of black pepper and serve four for lunch. You can add green onions to the onions if you like and if you have a dollop of sour cream you can stir that in, too, for a taste sensation. Call it fried potatoes. Here's another sneaky one.

48

Fish Pudding

Quarter a small onion and drop it into the bowl of your food processor, fitted with the steel blade. Give the onion one on-off as a warning and drop into the f.p. about 2 cups cooked fish, 1 tablespoon dried parsley, ½ teaspoon chervil, ½ teaspoon dry mustard, a splash of Worcestershire sauce, a generous grind of black pepper, 1 teaspoon salt, ¾ cup bread crumbs, 1 tablespoon lemon juice, and 2 egg yolks. Blend about 15 seconds. Beat 2 egg whites until stiff; fold the fish mixture gently into the egg whites. Turn the mush into a buttered 8″ × 4″ loaf pan, cover with foil, and put it in a 350° F. oven in a larger flat baking pan with 1 inch of boiling water in it. Bake 45 minutes, or until the pudding is firm but still moist. Serves four.

Onion
Cooked fish
Parsley
Chervil
Dry mustard
Worcestershire sauce
Black pepper
Salt
Bread crumbs
Lemon juice
Eggs, separated

"Soup and fish," said Sidney Smith, "explain half the emotions in life." I'm not sure I agree with that, though it does sound intriguing. I know there are some people who feel they could run the full gamut of emotions without ever having fish. My children are among them. Yet I feel that I would be denying them some of life's experience if I did not persevere with their association with fish, so I keep on. Even the French say that it is the sauce that makes the fish edible. Bearing that in mind, if you compose a casserole with a piquant (as they say) sauce, you should have something worth eating. Try this.

Compose-a-Casserole – Fish Division

Make a cream sauce, using 3 tablespoons butter or margarine to 3 tablespoons flour, and adding 1 cup fish stock (if you have it – or use clam juice, or instant chicken soup base, if you must) and 1 cup milk. Season with salt and pepper, ½ teaspoon chervil, and a dash of Worcestershire sauce. Heat and stir until well blended and cooked. Then blend in the grated rind and the juice of 1 lemon. Cook 1 package frozen chopped spinach according to directions, drain well. Then arrange the spinach in the bottom of a greased casserole dish. Combine 2 cups cooked rice with at least 1, preferably 2, cups flaked cooked fish, and half the sauce to moisten it. Arrange the fish mixture over the spinach; cover with the remaining sauce, poking holes in the mixture so the sauce will feel more at home. Bake in a 350° F. oven for 45 minutes until good and hot,

Butter
Flour
Fish stock or clam juice
Milk
Salt and pepper
Chervil
Worcestershire sauce
Lemon juice and rind
Spinach
Cooked rice
Cooked fish

or 1 hour if you've made it ahead and refrigerated it. If you're short on fish, of course, you can add mushrooms, or better, open a small can of salmon, drain, then mix it with your leftover fish. If you opt for the salmon, omit the chervil and substitute dill weed.

Shrimp in Aspic

Hot water
Lemon gelatin
Tomato juice
Vinegar
Worcestershire sauce
Tabasco
Cooked shrimp

This happened because the leftover shrimp (brought to a potluck pool party) were tiny and ill suited to a main course. But even 1 cup of little shrimp will do this nicely. Stir 1 cup hot water into a 4-serving-size package lemon gelatin until the gelatin is thoroughly dissolved (I count to 60) and stir in 1 cup tomato juice, 2 tablespoons vinegar, 1 teaspoon Worcestershire sauce, 2 drops Tabasco. Chill until thickened but not set; stir in the shrimp. Pour into a ring mould or into 6 individual moulds and chill until set. Unmould and serve on a bed of lettuce with mayonnaise and deviled eggs. Lunch.

You might think I'd classify a jambalaya under leftover ham, but I'm much more likely to make it with leftover shrimp even though the ham is left over, too. Any way you look at it, it's good.

Jambalaya

Onions
Green pepper
Salad oil
Chicken stock
Tomatoes
Rice
Bay leaf
Cooked shrimp
Cooked ham
Gumbo filé

Sauté 2 onions, diced, and ¼ cup chopped green pepper in 2 tablespoons salad oil until soft. Add 2 cups chicken stock and a 28-ounce can tomatoes or a 1-quart box of home-frozen. Add 1 cup raw rice and 1 bay leaf and bring to a boil. Reduce heat, cover, and cook until the rice is tender. Add 1 cup shrimp, or more if you have them, and 1 cup cut-up ham, or more if you want, and heat through. Stir in 1 tablespoon gumbo filé just before serving. Taste it (careful) and adjust the seasoning. Serve with hot corn bread and a raw zucchini salad or a tossed green salad. I was going to suggest okra, but if I were going to serve okra with it, I'd put the okra right into the jambalaya. Why not?

I've had leftover snails too. (If snails aren't seafood, don't tell me.) When I do snails at home somehow the arithmetic doesn't work out. It's all very well for restaurants: you order *escargots à la bourguigonne* and you get 6 snails and someone else washes the shells (I hope). At home you start with a can of 48 snails. You're having 6 people for dinner; 6 times 6 is 36. *Voila*, 12 leftover snails.

Snails Without Shells

Fry 4 slices bacon until crisp; crumble into a small saucepan. Add ½ cup red wine or sherry, 1 small onion, chopped, 2 cloves garlic, crushed, 1 tablespoon snipped parsley, and ¼ teaspoon thyme. Bring to a boil, stir down, and then cook at a low boil for 20 minutes. Add your leftover snails (12?) and 1 tablespoon brandy, and heat through. Spoon onto 2 slices garlic-buttered toast and serve yourself and your husband as a surprise hors d'oeuvre not more than 2 days after your dinner party.

Bacon
Red wine or sherry
Onion
Garlic
Parsley
Thyme
Snails
Brandy
Garlic-buttered toast

I never could understand people living over a fault in the earth's crust until we went to California a few years ago. Now I do. We decided we would, too, if someone asked us. I fell in love with California, especially San Francisco, especially the food. We ate sand dabs from the bay, clams from the seashore, crab at the Fisherman's Market, and sourdough bread by the pound. Among other things, we learned about and ate a Hangtown Fry. I hope I've got the story right. It seems a prospector staggered into Hangtown (now Placerville) during the gold rush with a sackful of gold. He went into the only café in town, dumped his gold on the table, and ordered the cook to cook him something, using only the most expensive ingredients because at last he could afford it. The two most expensive things in town were eggs and oysters so the cook created the first Hangtown Fry. I never got the recipe for it, but I thought of it a few months later when I had leftover oysters to use up.

Hangtown Bake

Beat 10 eggs with 1¼ cups cream, 1 teaspoon salt, and a good grinding of black pepper (¼ teaspoon?). Add 1 cup drained oysters. Fry 4 slices bacon until crisp; crumble into the bottom of a buttered 1½-quart casserole. Pour in the egg-oyster mixture and bake at 350° F. for 35 to 40 minutes or until set. Serves eight for brunch, with a yeast coffee cake and a green salad or a finger fruit salad.

Eggs
Cream
Salt
Black pepper
Oysters
Bacon

I have mentioned fish stock, but I said nothing about it in my chapter on soup. Fish stock is an evolution product; you get it when you have leftover fish and fish bones to cope with. My husband became very adept at butterflying smaller fish like brook trout for the barbecue, and I got all the bones and heads from that

51

operation. He also barbecued whole salmon and when we finished with it, the remains went into the fish stock pot. Another source of supply is gefilte fish stock. If you make your own gefilte fish, as I do, you'll know what I mean. Once you have a little court bouillon, as it is called, you need never do without. Keep it in the freezer. Thaw it when you want to poach fish. Oven-poaching is easy. Place the fish in a single layer in a shallow ovenproof baking dish, pour over it the court bouillon (barely cover the fish), and bake uncovered in a 375° F. oven for 25 minutes. Drain the fish and serve with hollandaise sauce – sole and turbot are simple and lovely this way. In time the court bouillon will shrink as you keep reusing it in this manner. Add a little water (or clam juice) and keep on using it. It gets richer and more jelly-like with each use. I use a Never-Ending Court Bouillon like this for a fall and winter season.

It's a good idea to disguise leftover fish as much as you can if you're cooking for children like mine. Sneak up on them with hamburger buns. (Call it a big mackerel attack?)

Surprise Buns (With Sole)

Parmesan cheese
Cheddar cheese
Celery
Onion
Cooked sole
Cream of mushroom
  soup
Buttered hamburger
  buns

Here's where you get to dirty two blades of your food processor. First, put the grating disc on and grate 2 tablespoons Parmesan cheese and ½ cup medium-sharp Cheddar cheese. Dump the cheese on a sheet of waxed paper and put the steel blade in. Throw some chunks of celery, enough to make ½ cup finely chopped, and ½ small onion into the bowl and give the vegetables one or two on-off circuits. Now dump in 1 can cream of mushroom soup, 2 cups (approximately) leftover cooked sole or other fish, and the cheese. A quick on-off should be enough to blend this so as to retain some texture. Glop the mixture into buttered hamburger buns (it should fill about 8 to 10 buns), and wrap each bun in foil. Heat in a 350° F. oven for 20 to 30 minutes. Lunch or supper. These freeze well and can be put directly from the freezer into a 375° F. oven – but they take about 45 mintues to thaw and heat through.

All right, it's homely fare, but it tastes good and it fills an empty space. Life isn't *cordon bleu* all the way. The whole business of cooking for others is a constant risk and challenge. I'm talking about taste, which is both arbitrary and intimate. If it should happen that another's taste buds react differently from mine, then that, as they say, is a matter of taste. I don't want to hear about it, though. I get enough feedback from my children. I begin to suspect that somehow, in spite of all my efforts, their taste buds really are different from mine.

How else, after all this time, could my two girls have developed a taste for well-done meat when they have never been exposed to anything but rare? But we have reached mutual decisions. One night at the dinner table – this was one of our more serious conversations – we all looked at each other and agreed we wouldn't eat Brussels sprouts again. And we haven't. We have had open rebellion about bean sprouts and I don't think any food is worth breaking up a family over. *Chacun à son goût*, as they say, and I hope so.

Surf-Broiled Sandwiches

These aren't really surf-broiled, but after a while making up names for things gets to you. I didn't know I had this talent; I guess it comes from years of subliminal instruction from women's magazines. Combine 1 cup leftover flaked cooked fish with ¼ cup each chopped celery and green pepper, ¼ teaspoon salt, 1 tablespoon lemon juice, and ⅓ cup mayonnaise. Spread on 4 slices toasted and buttered bread, and place on a cookie sheet. Beat 2 egg whites until stiff; fold in 2 tablespoons grated Parmesan cheese. Spread the egg-white mixture on the sandwiches, covering the filling. Sprinkle a little grated Cheddar cheese on each sandwich and bake 15 minutes at 350° F., until browned. Serves four.

Cooked fish
Celery
Green pepper
Salt
Lemon juice
Mayonnaise
Buttered toast
Egg whites
Parmesan cheese
Cheddar cheese

Garlic Shrimp

Make a garlic butter with lots of parsley and garlic: crush 6 or 8 cloves garlic into ¾ cup butter with 2 tablespoons snipped parsley; heat together in a small, not to say teeny, saucepan. Taste it (carefully – hot butter can burn your tongue) to see if you think it needs salt. Melted butter usually doesn't, but it's this thing about taste buds again. Bring me your poor tired but jumbo shrimp (6, 8, 10? I can't believe you'd have 12 of them!) and put them in a small flat ovenproof dish. Pour the melted garlic butter over them and bake 10 minutes in a 450° F. oven. Serve piping hot. Yum. In fact,

Garlic
Butter
Parsley
Jumbo shrimp

53

it's so good you might even consider doing it from scratch some-time so that each diner gets an individual serving of shrimp. Easier than snails bourguignonne and every bit as garlicky.

My Auntie Anna used to make fish balls with fresh fish, but I've adapted her recipe to make it possible with leftover cooked fish. Better keep calling them *fiski bollur* because some wag is bound to make a nasty comment.

Fiski Bollur

Onion
Cooked fish
Milk
Eggs, separated
Salt
Black pepper
Seasoned flour

Drop a small, quartered onion into the bowl of the tireless f.p. fitted with the steel blade, and give it a rush: one on-off should do it. Drop in 2 cups leftover cooked fish, ¼ cup milk, 2 egg yolks, 1 teaspoon salt, and ¼ teaspoon black pepper, and mix them. Beat 2 egg whites to a peak and fold in the fish mixture. Take heaping tablespoons of this glop, dip them in seasoned flour and shape into 12 balls, flattening them slightly. Chill at least an hour. Sauté in butter or margarine until they are golden brown, turning as you see fit. Serves six, unless someone wants more than 2 balls.

This is a lovely thing to do with leftover fish in the summertime.

Fish Mousse

Gelatin
Lemon juice
Onion
Boiling water
Mayonnaise
Sour cream or buttermilk
 and cottage cheese
Cooked fish
Dill weed
Parsley

Put 1 envelope plain gelatin in your blender or in the bowl of your food processor (steel blade) with 2 tablespoons lemon juice and allow to soften. Add 1 slice onion, and ½ cup boiling water and blend. Add ½ cup mayonnaise and 1 cup sour cream (you can substitute ½ cup buttermilk and ½ cup cottage cheese, or use all yogurt), and 2 cups leftover cooked fish – salmon, perch, sole, had-dock, etc. I have combined two different kinds of fish with great success. If you use all white fish, try substituting ½ cup tomato juice for half of the sour cream. It adds a different flavour and a nice colour to the mousse. Now, where were we? Still feeding the machine. Drop in 1 teaspoon dill weed and 1 tablespoon of parsley and season to taste. Give it a whirl. Pour into a mould – a fish mould if you have one – and chill until set. Unmould, put a stuffed olive slice where the eye should be if you used a fish mould, and serve on a bed of lettuce surrounded by sliced tomatoes and cucumbers. I like to serve hot pea pods with this, and baking powder biscuits. Nice for a cool dinner on a hot summer day.

I mentioned barbecuing salmon. Leftover salmon is beautiful. I can't think of any improvement on it the day after than just to serve it, cold, with mayonnaise and lettuce and sliced fresh tomatoes. But a whole salmon is large and it *does* go on, so here is something to do with it when it palls as a luncheon salad.

Salmon Pie

Combine 1 to 2 cups leftover diced cooked potatoes (or cook some, I'm easy), with ½ cup sour cream, 1 teaspoon dill seed, crushed in a mortar, 3 to 5 green onions, snipped, and your leftover salmon, forked into appetizing chunks. You should have about 2 cups of the salmon, but if you don't, throw in some mushrooms. Now add something to moisten this. Have you any leftover cream sauce, about 1 cup? Make it, or open a can of cream of mushroom soup, or shrimp soup. If you have any leftover peas or mixed veg. in the fridge you can throw them into this pie, too. Mix everything together lightly with a fork, season to taste, and turn into a deep pie pan or a shallow casserole. Top with a pastry topping and bake for 30 to 35 minutes at 400° F.

Cooked potatoes
Sour cream
Dill seed
Green onions
Cooked salmon
Cream sauce or cream of
  mushroom soup
Peas or mixed vegetables
Pastry topping

I suspect that after all this, the diehard fish-haters will say that I should buy and cook less fish so that I would have fewer leftovers to cope with. But that, of course, defeats the issue. If you feel that strongly about it, you should skip this chapter. Or feed the cat. Our cat loves leftover fish.

Chapter 4

Dairy: There Is No Such Thing As Too Much Sour Cream

I read a statistic somewhere that stated that eight hundred pounds of edible food are thrown into one family's garbage in a year. The statistic didn't mention which family that was and I never thought to ask. As for the person who weighed the edible garbage, people have strange jobs these days so why not? The point is that to someone of my generation, brought up on the Puritan work ethic and all the accompanying dicta that made me what I am today, it is a sin to throw out edible food. Waste not, want not. On the other hand, having struggled against a tendency to gain weight far too easily all my life, I will not urge my children to clean up their plates or take a second helping. So I cope with leftovers.

Strictly speaking, sour cream is not a leftover. Because I'm talking about sour cream, the kind you buy fresh in its own special container, and not soured cream, in a pitcher that was left at the back of the refrigerator and forgotten. But if you bought sour cream for some other purpose and have the rest of the carton to use up, or if sour cream is a permanent resident in your fridge, as it is in mine, and if you do agree that leftovers are omnipresent, then sour cream is a leftover because it's omnipresent.

Now we've established that, we can go on, but not too far or too fast. Stop at once for an easy, spur-of-the-moment hors d'oeuvre made possible by sour cream.

Sour Cream Dip

With a fork, whip 1 tablespoon good curry powder and a scant teaspoon salt into 1 cup sour cream. Put the mixture in a bowl and set it in the middle of a tray filled with raw vegetables: little flowerets of cauliflower, ditto of broccoli, cherry tomatoes, celery, green onions, green beans, asparagus tips, even thin slices of raw turnip, oh, and mushrooms, little button ones or slices of bigger ones. The French call these *crudités*, and they're great. But you can always use one leftover, cooked, artichoke leaf by leaf by leaf. This recipe makes a reasonable amount of dip for a small group; you can, of course, double it if you're having a party. If there is any leftover dip, stir in some mayonnaise and use it up as a sharp dressing for a wedge of lettuce, or as an optional sauce for a hot vegetable. By optional I mean don't pour it all over the vegetable. Pass it and let people who want it help themselves. The last thing you want is a pile of leftover cooked broccoli drenched in curried sour cream.

Curry powder
Salt
Sour cream
Raw vegetables

Sour cream is really the all-purpose cream. Everyone knows how good it is, served with or without chives or crisp bacon, spooned into a hot baked potato. It is also gorgeous with dill weed in it, spooned over hot tiny new potatoes. Or stirred into hashed brown potatoes.

Hashed Brown Potatoes with Sour Cream

I hope you know how to use an index because the classification of this cookbook by categories defies me. Perhaps I'll be sorry when I get to the leftover potatoes, but right now this seems to me to belong to sour cream. So will you please slice 3 small onions and fry them in ¼ cup bacon fat. Add 2 or 3 cooked potatoes, cut up, and stir and fry them gently until browned and piping hot. Just before serving stir in ½ to 1 cup sour cream; heat just long enough to let the sour cream get hot but not break up or curdle or anything disastrous like that. I do this purposely on a night when we're having liver because it softens the blow and takes the edge off some of the complaints. Blessed is sour cream for it is a peacemaker.

Onions
Bacon fat
Cooked potatoes
Sour cream

And it is also very good with sliced cucumbers, and a little salt and dill weed.

I make my horseradish for roast beef and for sandwiches with powdered horseradish mixed with sour cream and garlic salt to taste. Lots of sour cream and lots of garlic salt. But sour cream is equally adaptable to sweet tastes. Try whipping it with icing sugar and rum sometime to make a dip for washed but unhulled fresh strawberries. Beautiful. The leftover dip can go into your next frosting.

Sour cream goes with vegetables, fruits, fish, meat, and is indispensable in baking. The things it goes with make such wonderful leftovers to go with other things, it's like a chain reaction. Health-food addicts will recommend that you use yogurt instead of sour cream because it has fewer calories and you might live longer. I'm easy. Ask yourself, though, how long would you like to live without sour cream?

Any leftover will combine interestingly with sour cream (or yogurt) and some other leftover, like cooked meat, and make a quick luncheon casserole. Begin with mushrooms in sour cream, good by themselves, add meat, and you've won another day.

Mushrooms in Sour Cream

Mushrooms
Butter
Salt
Black pepper
Dill seed
Sour cream

Sauté 3 cups thick-sliced mushrooms in 2 tablespoons butter until they brown nicely and release some liquid, but don't let them get traumatic about it. Add salt and ground black pepper to taste, and 1 teaspoon crushed dill seed; stir in 1 cup sour cream. Heat gently until everything has successfully encountered everything else. Serve with a slotted spoon. I say slotted spoon because I don't like too much runny sauce on my plate, and besides you can use the sauce in something else. This makes a good side dish with a dinner meat or you can serve it on toast (garlic-buttered?) for a light lunch, heavier if you add some sliced hard-boiled eggs to it. Leftover sauce adds a beautiful taste to gravy, Bena Supa (see page 20), or practically any cream sauce.

Long before Quiche Lorraine became an "in" thing to cook, I used to make what I very simply titled Onion Pie which is simply quiche with onions. Now there are so many variations on the theme that the recipe hardly comes as any surprise, but in leaner times we were grateful for such humble fare.

58

Mushroom and Onion Pie

Sauté 3 large onions, sliced, in ¼ cup butter until they're soft and golden. Remove and drain. Turn ¼ pound fresh mushrooms, sliced, into the same butter and sauté gently, adding salt and pepper and a sprinkle of powdered mushrooms. Remove mushrooms and drain. Mix the mushrooms with the onions and stir in 3 eggs, beaten and mixed with 1 cup sour cream. Pour into 2 prebaked (8 minutes at 425° F.) pie shells and bake 10 minutes in a 425° F. oven, then 20 minutes at 350° F. If you make your pastry from scratch as I do, put 1 tablespoon crushed dill seed in the pie dough; it complements the mushrooms and sour cream. Or, if you want to omit the pastry entirely, lay a bed of the hot mushroom-onion mixture in a shallow casserole, crack as many eggs (gently) as desired over it, sprinkle with grated cheese and bake 10 or 15 minutes at 350° F.

Onions
Butter
Mushrooms
Salt and pepper
Powdered mushrooms
Eggs
Sour cream
Pie shells

Strictly speaking, the next recipe should not be in this book because I always buy the sour cream on purpose to make it. All the other things are made with sour cream left over from making this cake. But it's so good I couldn't bear not to include it.

Faigie's Chocolate Cake

With an electric mixer, cream ¾ cup butter with 1½ cups sugar till well blended and fluffy. Beat in 2 eggs, and if they're at room temperature, so much the better. In a separate bowl mix together 1¼ cups sour cream, ½ cup milk, and 2 teaspoons baking soda. Sift together 2¼ cups sifted flour and 1½ teaspoons baking powder. With the mixer on medium speed, add the flour to the butter-sugar mixture alternately with the sour cream mixture, making about 3 additions. Continue to beat on medium speed for a minute or so, scraping the sides of the bowl with a rubber scraper. Add 3 squares unsweetened chocolate, melted, and 1 teaspoon vanilla, and mix on low speed until well blended. Pour into 2 greased and floured 9-inch layer cake pans and bake 30 to 35 minutes in a 350° F. oven. This recipe doubles like a dream and you can freeze 2 layers for another day, or frost them both and give one to someone just home from the hospital or just moved or something traumatic like that. We'll frost it when we get to leftover egg whites (page 71).

Butter
Sugar
Eggs
Sour cream
Milk
Baking soda
Sifted flour
Baking powder
Unsweetened chocolate
Vanilla

59

And while we're on the subject of sour cream and Faigie, her coffee cake is great, too.

Faigie's Sour Cream Coffee Cake

Butter
Sugar
Eggs
Sour cream
Baking soda
Flour
Baking powder
Salt
Maraschino cherries
Brown sugar
Pecans

Cream together 1 cup butter and 2 cups sugar until fluffy. Beat in 4 eggs. In a separate bowl mix 2 cups sour cream with 2½ teaspoons baking soda. Sift together 3 cups flour, 4 teaspoons baking powder, and ¾ teaspoon salt; add to butter-sugar mixture in 3 additions, alternating with the sour cream mixture. Beat 2 minutes at medium speed of mixer, scraping the sides of the bowl with a rubber spatula until the batter is smooth and well blended. Generously butter a gugelhupf pan (if you have one) or a 10-inch tube pan. Arrange a pattern of halved maraschino cherries and pecans in the bottom of the pan and sprinkle generously with the filling (see below). Pour over the filling a layer of batter, about half of the total amount, then generously cover that with more filling. Top with the rest of the batter. Run a knife through the batter to swirl the filling through the coffee cake. Bake the cake 45 to 60 minutes in a 350° F. oven. Test it with a cake tester or toothpick before you remove it from the oven to make sure the insides aren't sticky. Cool 10 minutes, then invert on a wire cake rack. It's not only pretty, it's delicious.

Filling: mix together 1 cup brown sugar, firmly packed, with 1 cup finely chopped pecans. That's all. Invariably I have some filling left over and it's good in other things, particularly Apple Crips (see page 105).

Sour Cream Gingerbread

Corn oil
Sugar
Egg
Molasses
Sour cream
Sifted flour
Baking soda
Salt
Ginger
Cinnamon
Whipped cream

Mix ½ cup corn oil, ½ cup sugar and 1 egg in the blender or the f.p. bowl. Drop in ¾ cup molasses and 1 cup sour cream and blend it all. Sift together 2¼ cups sifted flour, 1 teaspoon baking soda, ½ teaspoon salt, 1 teaspoon ginger, and 1 teaspoon cinnamon. Pour the wet stuff from the blender into the dry stuff in the bowl and stir well to mix. Pour the batter into a 9-inch square buttered pan and bake in a 325° F. oven for 45 to 50 minutes. Serve warm, with sweetened whipped cream. And I'll tell you what to do with the leftover whipped cream a few pages farther along.

60

With the exception of chocolate cake and coffee cake, I have been known to substitute, or more likely mix, buttermilk and/or cottage cheese and/or yogurt with or for sour cream to make up my total amounts for whatever I want to make. Several years ago an ad for instant lemon pudding suggested blending 1 cup milk with 8 ounces cream cheese to form the basis of an instant cheesecake. Using that idea as my springboard, I went on to use lemon pudding in order to use up my heels of buttermilk, sour cream, cottage cheese, and yogurt. If there's more cottage cheese than anything, it's thick enough to be a cheesecake – if you scrape it into a graham cracker pie shell. But if there's more buttermilk or sour cream, it's still pudding consistency and better tasting than a pudding made with straight milk. Toss on some chocolate sprinkles. While we're on the subject, instant puddings come in very handy for using up leftover eggnog, chocolate milk, or hot chocolate (cold), also peanut butter (the last ½ cup in the bottom of the large economy jar), or an overripe banana. Just choose your flavour, and use your blender or food processor, following the package directions for the amount of liquid or semiliquid to use.

This mixing of sour cream, buttermilk, cottage cheese, and yogurt applies not only to instant puddings. Dill Bread is marvellous with sour cream and cottage cheese mixed, or with ⅓ cup each sour cream, cottage cheese, and buttermilk.

Sour Cream/Cottage Cheese/Buttermilk Dill Bread

Combine ½ cup sour cream, ½ cup cottage cheese (or buttermilk), 1 tablespoon instant onion, 2 tablespoons dill weed, 2 tablespoons corn oil, 1 egg, and ½ teaspoon baking soda. Sprinkle 1 package dry yeast over ½ cup warm water and let stand for 5 minutes, then stir well till the yeast is dissolved. Stir into the sour cream mixture and blend well. Sift into a bowl 3½ to 4 cups flour and 1 teaspoon salt. Pour the sour cream-yeast mixture over the flour and stir till the dough is stiff and ready to come out of the bowl. Knead briefly but viciously on a floured board, adding more flour if necessary. Put it in a greased bowl, turn once, cover with a damp dish towel, and let rise until double – about 1 hour. Shape into loaves and put in 2 greased loaf pans, 8"× 4"× 2½"; let rise again until double, about 45 to 55 minutes. Bake in a 350° F. oven for 40 to 50 minutes.

Sour cream
Cottage cheese or
  buttermilk
Instant onion
Dill weed
Corn oil
Egg
Baking soda
Yeast
Warm water
Flour
Salt

61

Auntie Anna's Bran Bread

Bran
Flour
Baking soda
Salt
Brown sugar
Raisins
Buttermilk

Dump 2 cups bran into a large bowl and sift over it 2 cups flour, 1 teaspoon baking soda, and 1 teaspoon salt. Mix in 1 cup brown sugar, firmly packed, and 1 cup raisins, then stir in 2 cups buttermilk. Mix well. Let stand half an hour in a warm place before putting it into a greased 9″ × 5″ × 3″ loaf pan; bake 30 to 40 minutes in a 350° F. oven.

And now I guess I have to tell you about buttermilk pancakes, which are not really made with leftover buttermilk. Other things are. But a friend of mine in Chicago says a friend of hers paid $75 for this recipe, which is supposed to have come from one of the old great hotels. Anyway, both of them have been giving the recipe away ever since to amortize the cost, and I'll give it to you. They are, immodestly, the best pancakes ever.

Buttermilk Pancakes

Flour
Baking soda
Salt
Buttermilk
Eggs
Honey
Butter
Cold water

Sift 2 cups flour with 2 teaspoons baking soda and 1 teaspoon salt. Lightly stir in 2 cups buttermilk. Drop 2 eggs into the batter, breaking the yolks. Melt together 2 tablespoons honey and 2 generous tablespoons butter and pour into the batter, stirring just enough to get everything together. Stir in 2 to 4 tablespoons cold water to thin the mixture; cook the pancakes on an ungreased but well-seasoned griddle.

Here's a good reason to have too much cottage cheese in the fridge.

Cottage Cheese Biscuits

Flour
Salt
Baking powder
Sugar
Shortening
Cottage cheese (or part sour cream)
Eggs

Sift together 3 cups flour, 1 teaspoon salt, 4 teaspoons baking powder, and 1 tablespoon sugar. Cut in ¼ cup shortening until the mixture is mealy. Blend together (in the blender or the f.p.) 2 cups cottage cheese (or use part sour cream) and 2 eggs. Pour this mixture into the flour mixture and stir it well. Turn it onto a floured board and knead it lightly. It seems a tough springy dough; bash it lovingly with the rolling pin and roll it out to a ¾-inch thickness. Cut into biscuit rounds and bake on a greased baking sheet for 12 to 16 minutes in a 450° F. oven. This makes 2½ dozen biscuit-sized biscuits, biscuit-round, that is, but almost twice as high as the usual biscuit. No danger of these hanging around.

Here's another completely unrelated recipe that happens with whatever combination of leftover dairy goodies you may have cluttering up your fridge.

Tuna Dip or Spread

Whether it's a dip or a spread depends on what you put into it. Empty the contents of a 7-ounce can of tuna, oil and all, into the blender or the food processor (steel blade) and throw ½ teaspoon hickory smoke seasoning on top of it, and 3 tablespoons or so cut-up pimiento and a quick grind of black pepper. Now drop your leftover cottage cheese, sour cream, or buttermilk in (total of a scant cup). Blend it well, then turn it into a pretty bowl surrounded either by potato chips, if it's a dip, or crackers, if it turns out to be a spread. It will be sort of pink if you blend in the pimiento. If you want more texture, stir in the pimiento, chopped by hand, after you have blended the other stuff. Or you can add or substitute a couple of tablespoons of chopped black or stuffed olives. This is a delightful, inexpensive, ever-ready canapé thing to have up your sleeve, or up your fridge's sleeve because you're bound to have a can of tuna on your shelf and if yours is like my fridge, you will always have some combination of the dairy ingredients.

Tuna
Hickory smoke seasoning
Pimiento
Black pepper
Cottage cheese, sour
  cream or buttermilk

And almost all these magic rules apply to leftover evaporated milk. You know, sometimes a recipe demands a half or a third of a cup and you are left with an open can in the fridge. It, too, can be poured into the instant pudding you're blending, the cream sauce you're stirring up, the cake batter or cookie dough or whatever. It is a wonderfully good moistener for hamburgers (¼ cup per pound of meat) or meat loaf, and our cat loves to drink it. No problem.

You could begin to suspect that I have a very large fridge. I do (plus two smaller ones). The kitchen fridge has a freezer in it the size of two ice-cube trays; all the rest is cold storage. The basement fridge is for the soup pot, large salads, extra grapefruit, and soda. The outside fridge is for soda, beer, and watermelon. I also have an upright freezer, the bottom basket of which is filled with soup bones. But I want to tell you about my cheese shelf. In the kitchen fridge. The joy of cheese is well known to cheese-lovers. But what about when the honeymoon is over? When you have a nasty little heel of Camembert, a superannuated dollop of Leiderkranz, an unyielding morsel of St. Paulin? Do you throw these out? *You* might, but I don't. Useless and unattractive though they seem, these bits of leftover cheese are the source of many of my greatest compliments.

Cheese Spreads

Butter
Brandy
Cream(y) cheese
Leftover cheese

Start with a strong blender or a sympathetic food processor, steel blade. Drop in 2 tablespoons soft butter and 2 to 4 tablespoons brandy, depending on how generous you feel and how much cheese you have to work with. If you're short on the leftover creamy cheese, add a 4-ounce package of plain cream cheese; if you have quite a combination of Brie, Camembert, Boursin, Nec Plus Ultra, etc., then you don't have to bother with the cream cheese. Now rummage through your cheese shelf and pick up all the bits and pieces and drop them in the blender, or the f.p. bowl. If some of the bits are very hard, grate them or cut them into small lumps so as to spare your blender motor; you can be as callous as you like with the food processor. Now turn on the motor and blend everything until you have a homogeneous cheese spread. Scrape it out of the container, and pack it into a good-looking crock with a cover. Refrigerate. Serve, at room temperature, with crackers, as one of the nicest hors d'oeuvres people ever wolfed. Warning: they will be angry because you cannot give them the recipe. The reason is, of course, that the recipe varies every time you make it, depending on what cheeses you had to use up. Stave off anger by giving your questioner a crock to take home. You *know* there's more where that came from.

Now about the options. If you are using only creamy cheeses and if you let them all come to room temperature, you can mix them in your mixer instead – not a bad idea if there's a lot to mix. You can drop some chopped walnuts or some chopped olives into the cheese spread for a pleasant variation. Sometimes, especially if there's a lot of it and especially if it has a decidedly blue cheese predominance, I toast some chopped blanched almonds (spread on a cookie sheet and baked till a toasty colour, 5 or 10 minutes, at 350° F.), spread the nuts on a sheet of waxed paper, turn a mound of cheese onto them, and roll and shape it into a nut-covered log.

64

This log can be refrigerated till needed or wrapped in waxed paper, then in plastic wrap and put in a plastic bag in the freezer. It makes a nice hostess gift to take to a friend's dinner party or a very acceptable do-ahead item for a cocktail party.

You can also use the cheese spread to make a spectacular but inexpensive hors d'oeuvre before a dinner party. Cut an unsliced loaf of white bread into crustless 1½-inch cubes. Generously spread your room-temperature cheese mixture on all sides of the cubes, put them on a baking sheet and pop them into a 350° F. oven until they are golden and bubbly – about 5 or 10 minutes. You can't spoil them – at least I never have. Serve hot, with cocktail napkins and pre-dinner drinks. You have to watch that some people don't eat too many or they won't have room for dinner!

Of all the ubiquitous leftovers, cheese and cheese spread are the most, next to soup. So when you already have a crock or two of cheese spread in the fridge, and a log or two in the freezer, start making cheese sauce.

Cheese Sauce

Make a basic cream sauce: 2 tablespoons butter to 2 tablespoons flour and 2 cups milk (or 1 cup milk and 1 cup cream). Season very lightly (if at all) with salt, because cheese is salty, and a few grains of cayenne pepper. Now the fun begins. If you want dinner out of it, first add 2 cups white wine to the sauce. Then stir in shredded or cut-up cheese – the Cheddars and the milder cheeses like Muenster, Swiss, and St. Paulin are better to use than the sharp and/or creamy ones. Use about a pound of cheese altogether, or 4 cups shredded. Gently, gently stir in all this cheese to make a really thick sauce – so thick it has trouble dripping off the spoon. Don't stop stirring. Stir in 2 tablespoons kirsch, and transfer the sauce to a fondue pot over a flame. Serve it at table as a simple Saturday night Fondue Supper, with hunks of French bread and more white wine to drink and a salad and a bowl of fruit. You can, of course, offer other things to dip in the cheese sauce besides bread. Shrimp would be nice, or a few leftover wieners cut in 1-inch slices, or garlic sausage, also in 1-inch slices.

But if you omit the wine and Kirsch and only add 1 cup shredded cheese and maybe 1 teaspoon Worcestershire sauce, then you have a perfectly adaptable cheese sauce to dump in lots of casseroles, and not only macaroni. A cheese sauce like this is a good

Butter
Flour
Milk
Salt
Cayenne pepper
White wine
Cheese
Kirsch

way to use up leftover cooked vegetables; it's great with cauli-flower and broccoli, and a boon to mixed vegetables. Or you can thin the sauce with more milk and maybe a bottle of beer just for fun, but stir carefully and watch that it doesn't curdle; serve it as Cheese Soup. Or you can beat in 3 or 4 eggs and ½ teaspoon nutmeg and pour it over partially cooked bacon or bits of leftover ham in a prebaked (8 minutes at 425° F.) pie shell; bake it 45 minutes in a 375° F. oven for the fastest quiche this side of Switzerland. Or you can fry up a mess of sliced onions, and I mean a mess of them, say 8 or 10 large onions, in ½ cup butter, and use up all the cheese in the fridge to make a *really* thick sauce. Add the sauce to the onions, turn into a loaf pan or casserole, and bake it for 30 minutes at 350° F. I don't know what you'd call this, but it's awfully good. If you like cheese and onions. Onion Cheese Pot?

Sometimes you have leftover cheese that proves to be intractable. You *know* it will break the blender motor if you try to add it to a cheese spread, and it would make the spread lumpy and unco-operative, anyway. If you have a food processor, the cheese will achieve gratedness with ease. Combine it with bread crumbs or not, as you prefer; sprinkle it with lavish abandon over the tops of casseroles before you put them in the oven. You can combine different cheeses in their grated form; the oven will bring them together in warm bubbly companionship. You can make lattice strips of the softer cheeses for casserole toppings, but if I'm going to use lattice strips I lay them on top of bacon slices in quiche. Who ever said Quiche Lorraine had to be made with Swiss cheese? Not me. One of the nicest ones I ever made used up a neglected piece of onion cheese, and it was sensational. And then, of course, there are always sandwich fillings, but I think I'll talk about that when I get to leftover bread. We must get on to blue cheese now because a little goes a long way and a lot goes even further.

Here's a specialty I made up which I find brings both cheese and mushroom lovers to their knees.

Blue Cheese Mushroom Bites

Mushrooms
Blue cheese

Wash and wipe carefully large mushrooms and remove the stems without breaking the caps. Chop the stems finely into a bowl and mash them with an equal volume of blue cheese, or leave it all for the friendly f.p. to do. It's up to you whether you want to go on-off

66

a couple of times and retain some texture, or to let the motor run for 5 or 10 seconds. Heap the mixture back into the mushroom caps, cover and chill for at least an hour before serving. These are fantastic canapes, and they sure use up the blue cheese!

When we were young and poor we liked to have parties with friends, but couldn't afford much in the way of exotic food. I haven't thought of this for years, but it is still a good, inexpensive way to feed people an evening snack, and you can use up leftover cheese to do it.

Cheese Oven Bread

Slice a loaf of rye bread almost through to the bottom crust and separate the slices with your fingers – wide enough to slip between each bread slice a slice of sharp Cheddar cheese and a slice of raw onion. Push the loaf back together as well as you can – it will be so loaded with cheese and onion it will look like an expanded accordion file. Wrap it in aluminum foil and put it in a 350° F. oven for half an hour (longer if you forget it), until the cheese is gorgeously melted into the bread and onion. Serve in a basket and let people tear out their own hunks of bread and cheese. And have plenty of napkins and dill pickles to go with it. A thought: if you have a lot of blue cheese around, make it with blue cheese instead of Cheddar.

Rye bread
Cheddar cheese
Onion slices

Cheese Diamonds

If you *still* have a lot of cheese lying around, then you're like us: you buy too much cheese. Cheese Diamonds are a good way of using the last of your pastry as well as the last of your cheese, and they rarely last till the next day. You have just baked a quiche or an apple pie or tarts – something, anyway, with pastry – and you have a small ball of pastry, all warm and ready to roll and not enough for another pie or even a pie shell. Roll it out on your floured board, spread it with soft butter, and sprinkle a generous amount of grated cheese all over it. Then fold all the sides in on themselves until you have a neat little rectangular package. Flour the board again, turn the package once or twice in the flour and roll it out very thinly. Cut it into diamond shapes with a pastry cutter, lift the diamonds and place on an ungreased baking sheet.

Pastry dough
Butter
Cheese

Bake in the oven you put your pie or quiche in for about 8 minutes or until the diamonds are golden brown.

Now it's about butter. You'll usually find a little bowl of garlic butter in my fridge. I feel about garlic and garlic butter the way I feel about sour cream: there's no such thing as too much. And if you haven't any left over, get some. You have leftover garlic butter when you made more than your loaf of garlic bread could accommodate, and it's a good thing. Sometimes you have leftover garlic butter from stuffing snail shells and that's even better because it has wine in it, and shallots, and good things like that. But my everyday garlic butter isn't bad and I guess I'd better tell you about it.

Garlic Butter

Garlic or garlic salt
Butter
Parmesan cheese
Poultry seasoning
Parsley

In the old days, B.F.P., I would use lavish amounts of garlic salt stirred into soft butter as the base for my garlic butter. Now I drop several – say 7 or 8 to start – garlic cloves into the food processor bowl (steel blade) with 1 cup butter, 1 tablespoon grated Parmesan cheese, 1 teaspoon poultry seasoning, and 2 tablespoons dried chopped parsley – or fresh – and let her rip. A friend of mine calls my garlic bread Green Bread because of the parsley in the butter, but no one ever turned away from it.

So you have a jar of it left over in your fridge. Drop a tablespoon of it into a sizzling-hot frying pan to cook a fast-fry steak. Melt ½ cup of it and pour it over 2 pounds barely thawed fish fillets, top them with extra grated Parmesan cheese and bake them 30 minutes in a 375° F. oven. Substitute it for, or add it to, the unseasoned butter or margarine you sauté onions and things in for most of the compose-a-casseroles you make. (Incidentally, melted butter keeps longer and better if you clarify it.)

Melt it and pour it over leftover shrimp to heat up in an oven for an instant Garlic Shrimp (page 53). Or spread it on hot toast for a great accompaniment to some luncheon cold cuts. Put a cold spoonful of it on a hot steak or hamburger just before serving. And stay away from the theatre, football, and hockey games, and your dentist. It's only fair.

You can't make an omelet without breaking eggs, goes the old saying, but no one ever said *when* you had to break the eggs. I

68

have said that using up leftovers is like following a chain reaction, with one good thing leading to another. With eggs it's more like a vicious circle. I never seem to end up even on whites or yolks and the more good things that get led to, the more of one or the other I have to lead on with. Don't put all your eggs in one basket, warns the proverb, but this doesn't apply to egg whites. I discovered very early in life that it's the only way to stay sane, as a matter of fact. Our pediatrician believed in starting our babies on egg yolks at a very early age (four weeks), but either he neglected to tell me when to start the whites or I neglected to ask; somehow, they never ate a whole egg until they were a year old. My character and my temperament forbade me to throw out the egg whites, so for eleven months, four times, I coped with egg whites.

The way to do it is one at a time. You keep a covered plastic container in the fridge and add egg whites as you acquire them. You can store them like this up to 10 days, then make a cumulative angel food cake on the tenth day (10 days equals 1¼ cups of egg whites, which is the standard amount for such a cake). If you do not have an inexorable cumulative drive you will not, of course, acquire your egg whites quite so fast, in which case you can freeze them. Simply put a covered plastic container in the freezer and let nature take its course. Add an egg white whenever you come across one, dropping it on the frozen surface of earlier egg whites. Cryogenics for eggs. When you are ready to use them, remove the container from the freezer and allow the whites to thaw at room temperature. Go ahead and use them for anything you wish. I have kept egg whites successfully in the freezer for 2 months or more.

If you do not have the patience to collect enough egg whites for an angel food cake or you'd rather have cookies, why not whip up a batch of meringues the next time you have a dry day and the wind is blowing from the east. Tip: drop in a cup of chocolate chips.

Ramos Fizz

I think the recipe originated in New Orleans, but we first discovered it in San Francisco. It's a nice Easter brunch drink if you have as many eggs lying around in various forms as we do at Easter time. But any time is nice. For each drink you need ½ teaspoon lemon juice, ½ tablespoon sugar, 2 ounces gin or vodka, 1 teaspoon orange juice, and 1 egg white. Blend these ingredients in the blender with cracked ice (3 ice cubes' worth) and strain into a juice

Lemon juice
Sugar
Gin or vodka
Orange juice
Egg white(s)
Cracked ice
Soda water

glass. Fill with cold soda water to top it off and serve with praise and thanksgiving.

This is to use up coloured hard-boiled Easter eggs.

Easter Eggs on Toast

Butter
Flour
Cream
Chicken stock
Salt and pepper
Worcestershire sauce
Egg yolks
Hard-boiled eggs
Buttered toast

Make a thick rich beautiful cream sauce: 3 tablespoons butter to 3 tablespoons flour, one cup cream, and 1½ cups chicken stock, salt and pepper and Worcestershire sauce to taste. Stir in a couple of egg yolks – I'm sure you can spare them. Add peeled whole hard-boiled eggs, allotting 1 or two per consumer, and heat gently until the eggs are heated through. Serve on buttered toast with green peas and a salad. Or you can stir 1 tablespoon curry powder into the butter along with the flour and cook it a bit before you add the liquid. Slice the hard-boiled eggs in this case so that each slice will pick up that lovely colour and flavour. Or if you want to do this at some other time of year when hard-boiled eggs are not a problem, substitute whole mushrooms, barely subdued by a preparatory sauté in a couple of tablespoons of butter, for half of the eggs and season the sauce with 1 teaspoon crushed tarragon.

After Easter I also make egg and onion sandwiches and deviled eggs and eat peeled whole hard-boiled eggs out of hand (with the whites all streaked with strange colours which have bled through cracks in the shells during the dipping) until the children are thoroughly fed up with hen eggs.

Turn back the chronological clock now. The following recipe happened as a result of some Christmas cooking. Every Christmas I bake Christmas breads for gifts: stollens, gugelhupfs, bundt-kuchens, julecages, panettones, etc. One year I tried a *potica*, an Italian coffee cake that has a filling of raisins, nuts, honey, and lemon within the sweet dough. Somehow or other, there was too much filling oozing out between the folds of the bread and I wasn't going to force it. I have cleaned many an oven as a result of overenthusiasm at the forcing-table. So I baked the bread with as much filling as it could bear and faced the rest of the filling with my usual sense of adventure and challenge, not to say dismay. The result of my ingenuity was taken to a Christmas meeting; at coffee time, the ladies begged me for the recipe. Then, of course, I had to figure out what I had done. I want you to know I'm still talking about egg whites. If I hadn't had any in the fridge this thing would never have happened.

Bar Nothing Cookies

Cream together ½ cup soft butter and ½ cup brown sugar, firmly packed; beat in 1 cup sifted flour until well blended. Easiest thing in the world to do in the food processor, steel blade. Pack the mixture into the bottom of a 13″×9″ pan, pressing the dough evenly with your fingers. Bake 10 minutes at 350° F. Snip 1 cup raisins with scissors and combine with ½ cup chopped nuts and ¼ cup honey and 1 tablespoon butter melted together. Or (don't bother washing the bowl) drop the raisins, nuts, honey and soft butter into the f.p. and let the steel blade make sense of it all, adding one teaspoon grated lemon rind. Fold into 3 (or 4) egg whites, beaten stiff, and pile this mixture on top of the baked layer. Bake 25 minutes at 350° F.

Butter
Brown sugar
Flour
Raisins
Chopped nuts
Honey
Butter
Lemon rind
Egg whites

Finally we are getting around to the frosting to top that sour cream chocolate cake I told you about (page 59). Still using egg whites.

Faigie's Frosting

Put 2 cups brown sugar, packed, 4 egg whites (preferably at room temperature), and 6 tablespoons cold water in the top of a double boiler and beat like mad over boiling water until the mixture is really stiff and holds a peak. This amount will frost 2 double layer cakes, but may easily be halved if you only baked one. I prefer to use up strawberry jam or grape jelly as the filling between the layers and reserve this fluffy stuff for the outside. Melt 2 squares semisweet chocolate with 1 teaspoon butter over hot water; stir them together and drip this mixture over the cake to form 5 or 6 parallel lines. Then with a toothpick draw 5 or 6 parallel lines at right angles to the chocolate lines and you get a very pretty pattern. It looks like a magazine illustration, as a matter of fact, and convinces your children that you are the best mother in the whole world.

Brown sugar
Egg whites
Cold water
Semisweet chocolate
Butter

Cantaloupe Surprise

Halve and remove the seeds from 3 cantaloupes and place them in a large baking pan filled with ice cubes. Fill the centres of the halves with hard vanilla ice cream. Cover the ice cream and the top edges of the cantaloupe with 3 or 4 egg whites that have been

Cantaloupes
Vanilla ice cream
Egg whites
Sugar

beaten stiff and sweetened with ½ cup sugar. Place the pan in a 500° F. oven for 5 or 6 minutes or until the meringues are golden brown. Serve immediately.

Egg yolks. An egg yolk or two in cream sauces or soups makes them velvety smooth, and rich too. Hollandaise sauce is something you'll always have lots of left over because you keep on using up leftover egg yolks to make it.

If there's too little Hollandaise left over for next time, stir in some (leftover) unsweetened whipped cream and you'll have mousseline sauce – which is also gorgeous with asparagus, but out of this world with fish! And in a pinch I have stirred in sour cream (have I *mentioned* sour cream?) I don't know what this is called, but it's good.

Sometimes, when a birthday or special occasion forces you to separate a whole lot of eggs on purpose for an angel food cake, you come by a large number of egg yolks. Egg yolks are not as patient about waiting around as egg whites are. You're supposed to cover egg yolks with cold water and keep them in a tightly closed container, but they get kind of yecchy this way and the only thing to do with them then is to drop them into a cookie dough. Better keep them golden, round, unscathed, and unwatered, and make a pie.

Custard Pie

Egg yolks
Sugar
Salt
Nutmeg
Evaporated milk
Rum
Pie shell

Beat 7 or 8 egg yolks till broken and fraternal. Beat in ¾ cup sugar, ½ teaspoon salt, ¼ teaspoon grated nutmeg, a 16-ounce can evaporated milk, and 2 tablespoons rum. Pour into a 9-inch pie pan lined with unbaked pastry and shove it in a 450° F. oven for 12 minutes. Reduce the heat to 350° F. and finish it off for 25 to 30 minutes. Nice to grate a little extra nutmeg on top before you bake it. It looks pretty and tastes better. If you're in a hurry or want to skip some calories, forget the pie shell. Pour the custard into a 1½-quart glass casserole and set it in an inch of boiling water in a pan in the 350° F. oven. Bake for 30 to 35 minutes or until a silver knife thrust into the custard comes out clean.

But if you're tired of all that cooking, then just simmer the egg yolks in a little water till hard-cooked, or cook them without water in the top of a double boiler, and push them through a sieve. Then you can sprinkle this stuff on top of vegetables – I think this

72

is called à la Goldenrod – or into a salad, or on top of casseroles (when you run out of grated cheese) with bread crumbs and dots of butter. I'm not guaranteeing the reaction you'll get from your children, mind you. Or stir it into other stuff you're mashing up for sandwich fillings. And speaking of sandwich fillings, if you have a child who balks at a breakfast egg you cooked, don't throw out that egg either. Mash it up with sandwich spread, mix it with crumbled cooked bacon or tuna or whatever, and hide it between 2 slices of buttered bread for lunch. The trick is to get rid of it quickly.

I also use uncooked yolks for frosting. If I don't have a yolk around I use a whole egg.

Never-Ending Frosting

Drop 2 yolks (or 1 egg) into a mixer bowl with ¼ cup soft butter or margarine, 2 tablespoons cream, and 1 teaspoon vanilla. Sift in 1 cup icing sugar and start the motor. Beat the frosting like mad, adding more sugar until you achieve the desired buttercream consistency. By this time you will have far more frosting than you need for the cake you are going to frost, but this stuff keeps beautifully in a covered container in the fridge and the next time you need to frost a cake, it's called instant.

Egg or egg yolks
Butter
Cream
Vanilla
Icing sugar

I never complain if I have one lone egg yolk waiting to be remembered in the fridge because I always remember it for something, preferably within 2 days. Mixed with a tablespoon of water and painted on a meat pie pastry it makes the most beautiful glaze, the kind that makes you seem like a professional cook. Similarly with one egg white: beat that with a tablespoon of water and brush it on bread before baking; it gives the bread a high hard gloss, suitable for photographing or eating. Nothing ever stays lonely for very long in my fridge.

Chapter 5

Vegetables: Ratatatooey!

Given their druthers, most males would rather not eat vegetables. They seem by nature to be the more carnivorous of the human pair. Cut-up plants, whether cooked or raw, don't hold much appeal for them. Most children, I'm sorry to say, are not unlike the average adult male in their aversion to vegetables. However, they can be brought along. I keep reminding myself of this fact as I watch our older son ignore the cauliflower and eggplant and wolf his meat. I will allow my children to dislike only a few specific foods, and I leave the choice up to them. I will not allow a total boycott of an entire class of foods, such as vegetables; it smacks of bigotry and intolerance instead of being an interesting foible. A specific dislike is possibly dictated by body chemistry, which I respect; a carte blanche abstinence from greens is caused by prejudice and must be outgrown.

Given that basic premise, we will begin with artichokes. Our children can't remember a time when they didn't eat and enjoy artichokes. If I want to have a leftover artichoke lying around, I either have to buy a lot extra or arrange to have one or two of the kids invited out to dinner after the artichokes have begun to cook. Still, it's worth some extra planning because there are some great things you can do with a cooked artichoke.

Artichokes Empress

Cooked artichoke
  bottom(s)
Poached egg(s)
Vinaigrette sauce

My husband and I had this for openers at the Empress Restaurant in London. It's easy to reproduce at home and makes an impressive introduction to any meal. You need 1 artichoke bottom per serving and 1 poached egg, neatly trimmed and chilled. Place the egg on the artichoke bottom and pour over it a couple of tablespoons of vinaigrette sauce or, if you prefer, some warm hollandaise sauce. Gorgeous. It can also be made with canned artichoke bottoms and is a lifesaver for a spur-of-the-moment party. I guess I'd better tell you how I make the sauce.

Vinaigrette Sauce

Pour ¼ cup wine vinegar into ½ cup salad oil (corn, olive, your choice) and add ½ teaspoon each salt, dry mustard, and black pepper. Stir well. Optionally you can add 1 teaspoon snipped chives and 1 tablespoon minced parsley.

Wine vinegar
Salad oil
Salt
Dry mustard
Black pepper
Chives
Parsley

You have to have palate aforethought to have enough artichokes left over to make this one.

Artichokes and Mushrooms

Take 3 or 4 cups chopped artichoke bottoms, the amount depending on how many artichokes you were able to buy cheap, cook in quantity, or save from your consumers, and mix the artichokes with 1 or 2 cups chopped fresh mushrooms. Let's hope you have a total of at least 3 cups of the combined vegetables. Add 1 teaspoon chopped chives, fresh or freeze-dried, 1 teaspoon dried parsley, ½ teaspoon each dill weed and salt, and ¼ teaspoon ground black pepper; mix in ½ cup cream. Turn into a buttered casserole and dot with 1 tablespoon butter. Bake briefly – 20 minutes – at 350° F.

Cooked artichoke
 bottoms
Mushrooms
Chives
Parsley
Dill weed
Salt
Black pepper
Cream
Butter

Artichokes are great companions. They complement many different tastes, a quality that may be inferred from the number of accompanying sauces that may be served with them. The Greeks lean to a mustardy-lemon taste with theirs, the French to a vinaigrette, I bend quite a lot toward melted butter, *not* clarified (too bland), and I know people who would rather fight than switch from hollandaise sauce. But I know only one person who would turn away from the delectable garlic-laden Provençal mayonnaise known as *aioli* sauce. (It's heavenly with new potatoes, cherry tomatoes, cauliflower, broccoli, asparagus, shrimp, lobster, and fish as well as artichokes.) That person happens to be so violently allergic to garlic she has to go to the hospital if her salad bowl is rubbed with it. Imagine what would happen to her if she ate Aioli Sauce.

Aioli Sauce

Garlic
Lemon juice
Egg yolks
Salt
Salad oil

Peel and drop in your patient blender or eager f.p. the cloves from one entire bud of fresh garlic, 10 to 14 in all. This is another job that the blender can do, but that the food processor does superbly. Add 3 tablespoons lemon juice and turn on the motor to crush the garlic and blend it with the lemon juice. Add 3 egg yolks and ½ teaspoon salt and blend again. Now slowly pour in 1 cup salad oil, with the motor running, until you have a creamy thick mixture the texture of mayonnaise – because that is what this is, a mayonnaise with conviction.

This sauce will help use up asparagus, too, if you're among friends.

Asparagus, like artichokes, is very adaptable. If you're tired of asparagus and cheese on toast, then beat 2 or 3 of your leftover egg whites until stiff, blend in ½ cup grated Cheddar cheese and pile it on asparagus and toast. Pop it into a 375° F. oven for 6 or 7 minutes and serve.

A couple of spears of leftover asparagus need never be wasted. They can be cut into a green salad for several people, or laid on a lettuce leaf and decorated with a dollop of mayonnaise and a strip of pimiento for one. Sometimes, though, for goodness knows how many diverse reasons, you will have more than 2 or 3 leftover spears. Maybe there was a good buy on asparagus in the store, but it looks too spindly to serve by itself. That's one reason and a good excuse to make a quickie.

Asparagus Pie

Cooked asparagus
Pie shell
Cheddar cheese
Eggs
Cream
Milk
Nutmeg
Salt
Worcestershire sauce

Lay spears of cooked asparagus to cover the bottom of a pre-baked (8 minutes at 425° F.) 9-inch pie shell, and sprinkle with 1 cup grated Cheddar cheese. Beat 4 eggs with 1 cup cream and 1 cup milk. Grate in ¼ teaspoon nutmeg, add ½ teaspoon salt and splash in some Worcestershire sauce (½ teaspoon). Strain over the filling and put the pie in a 375° F. oven to bake 40 minutes or until the custard is set and a knife comes out clean.

A favourite Mennonite recipe is bean salad, which lends itself easily to second appearances.

76

Bean Salad

Basically the bean salad recipe calls for 1 can each cut green beans, cut wax beans, lima beans, and kidney beans, all drained (drain the vegetable juices into your current soup pot — no sense throwing all those vitamins down the drain). Put the vegetables in a glass or pottery bowl and add 1 green pepper, seeded and cut in narrow strips, and 1 Spanish onion, sliced very thinly and the rings separated. Toss with your favourite vinaigrette or French dressing, cover, refrigerate, and allow to ripen for at least 24 hours before serving — the salad improves with age. Now some cooks add a can of chick peas to this as well, and some add chopped celery. But you can see how readily this adapts to leftovers. The proportions really don't matter that much, either, as long as there's an interesting variety of munchable beans. So govern yourself according to your leftovers: green and wax beans you will have in abundance at the height of the season, lima beans are left over when you cooked too many from a frozen bagful, and kidney beans are, too, if you have a cup or so too many for a chili con carne. But even a one-bean salad, wax or green, will do for lunch. Call it vinaigrette and roll the *r* a bit as you say it so people will know you're being very French and frugal.

I'll tell you my secret with this salad, but it's really my secret with any salad. I knew it would come up sooner or later. My secret is based on a Spanish proverb: "Four persons are wanted to make a salad: a spendthrift for oil, a miser for vinegar, a counselor for salt, and a madman to stir it all up." That, and another rule of thumb: as you pour, draw a circle and a cross with the oil and a cross with the vinegar over the greens in the bowl. Then judiciously shake and rattle the seasonings in: your favourite seasoning salt, black pepper, dill weed. Dill is good with the beans, tarragon is better with mushrooms. The only time I couldn't do it by feel and taste like this was when I was pregnant. What's thirty-six months out of a lifetime? Three years of bad salads, that's what my husband would have told you. So he and the older children learned how to make salad.

Green beans
Wax beans
Lima beans
Kidney beans
Green pepper
Spanish onion
Vinaigrette or French
 dressing

Heavenly Father, bless us,
And keep us all alive,
There's ten of us to dinner
And not enough for five.
　　　　　— Hodge's Grace

This seems to happen most frequently on a Sunday when we're having a large roast beef and a fit of hospitality suddenly threatens to stretch further than the roast. That's when we cooks of leftovers swing into action. Don't look upon this situation as a problem; look on it as a way to empty the fridge. Whip out one of your crocks of cheese or liver pâté and some crackers and fill a plate with Cheese Diamonds (page 67). Give your guests a little something before they hit the table and it will help stop the gap your now-meagre roast must fill. Put your ever-ready soup pot on the stove and serve soup first – and throw some croutons in it. Make garlic bread (or pull one from the freezer), or do a fast garlic toast, or baking powder biscuits or popovers (I don't like Yorkshire pudding). Add a course. Add a vegetable. Throw more potatoes and carrots around the roast. Slice the roast thin. French the green beans. Enrich the dessert.

The reason I brought up this problem was the green beans. I have an electric bean-Frencher but even when I didn't I used to French them by hand with the other end of my floating-blade potato peeler. Somehow Frenched beans go a lot further than un-Frenched. In fact, after all your bulwarks thrown up to stave off hunger at your overpopulated dinner party (you never *meant* it to be a party!), guess what's left over?

Green Bean Casserole

Boiling water
Tuna
Cream of mushroom
 soup
Milk
Cooked green beans
Eggs, separated
Cheddar cheese
Parmesan cheese

Pour boiling water over the contents of two 7-ounce cans tuna in a sieve, then flake the fish into a casserole; dump in 1 can cream of mushroom soup and ⅓ cup milk. Stir in 1 to 1½ cups cooked green beans, then pop into a 350° F. oven for 10 minutes. Beat 4 egg yolks and add ¼ cup grated Cheddar cheese and ¼ cup grated Parmesan cheese. Beat 4 egg whites till stiff and fold into the yolk-cheese mixture. Pile on the tuna-green bean mixture and bake another 30 minutes. This will serve four for dinner or six for a light lunch.

But I know there are times when you're in a hurry and you have these cooked green beans in the fridge or wax beans or both and you don't want to make a production out of it, you just want to reheat them and get rid of them. Well, just for my sake why don't you heat them in a tablespoon of that nice garlic butter you always have in your fridge now? Or stir in a handful of shelled sunflower

78

seeds before you serve them, or ¼ cup toasted slivered almonds (there are some on the shelf in a jar left over from making a Cheese Nut Log in the previous chapter).

And not to forget what has gone before in this book, you can also add these vagrant beans to a ham casserole, a salmon pie, a lamb pie, or a beef stew. Cross-index your thinking.

I never mind giving away a recipe, but I hate to meet myself everywhere. This happened a couple of years ago to a recipe I let loose, and I shudder to think of it now because I met it at every party and buffet and church bazaar and even an Italian night at the local art gallery. Try to use a little discretion.

Antipasto

Throw leftover cooked green and/or wax beans and carrots, cut small, into a large bowl – the vegetables should total 1 to 1½ cups. Add 1 can button mushrooms, drained (drain the liquid into the soup pot), up to ½ cup each stuffed olives and sweet mixed pickles (cut them up if they're large), and 2 or 3 tablespoons chopped ripe olives, if they're lying around. Keep going with a 7-ounce can tuna (including the oil), a 10-ounce bottle chili sauce, or whatever is left in the bottle you have plus ketchup and/or tomato sauce to make up the difference. The point of this whole operation is to get rid of your leftover vegetables and at the same time empty the door shelves of your fridge and clean out your condiment cupboard. It's a great thing to do *after* a big party to use up the heels of all the goodies you bought for the party. Now add a few little cocktail onions (there's another jar gone), 1 tablespoon prepared horseradish, and 1 teaspoon Worcestershire sauce. Chop celery to total 1 cup and throw that in with the juice of 1 lemon. Now mush it all together, but gently; it's doing you a favour. Put it in a couple of large covered jars or crocks in the fridge to allow these newfound acquaintances to ripen into friendship. To serve, mound on a lettuce leaf as a fork-food antipasto, or serve it in an attractive small bowl surrounded by crackers to pile it on. It's very good, and has been known to cause addiction.

Cooked green and/or
  wax beans
Cooked carrots
Button mushrooms
Stuffed olives
Sweet mixed pickles
Ripe olives
Tuna
Chili sauce
Cocktail onions
Horseradish
Worcestershire sauce
Celery
Lemon juice

I always thought the French word *macédoine* was a nicer way to describe mixed vegetables than mixed vegetables. "Mixed" sounds rather careless and haphazard, and you can't ever afford to be careless with leftovers – especially vegetables, as they do mount up.

Macédoine En Croute

Bread
Cooked vegetables
Onion
Butter
Flour
Milk
Cheddar cheese
Seasonings
Croûtes

Push de-crusted buttered slices of bread into large muffin cups and toast them in a 350° F. oven until crisp and golden. Now mix all the amenable leftover vegetables you can find in your fridge; by amenable, I mean I wouldn't put beets in because they will ruin your colour scheme. But try green beans, wax beans, peas and carrots, cauliflowerets (if they were cooked tender-crisp and not mushy), corn niblets, and maybe a tablespoon of chopped green onions. Make a cheese sauce: start with a white sauce (1 tablespoon butter to 1 tablespoon flour and 1 cup milk), stir in ½ to ¾ cup grated Cheddar cheese and season to taste; cook and stir until thickened and ready. Pour the vegetables into the sauce and allow them to heat. To serve, put a warm croûte on each plate and spoon the vegetables in sauce into it.

If by chance you don't have enough bread to use up to make this croûte business worthwhile, then use your vegetables with a bread of your own making – like this.

Vegetables with Biscuit Rolls

Butter
Flour
Milk
Cheddar cheese
Salt and pepper
Cooked vegetables
Biscuit dough
Parsley or watercress

Make a cream sauce: 4 tablespoons butter or margarine to 4 tablespoons flour and 2 cups milk. Stir and cook and add 1½ to 2 cups grated Cheddar cheese; stir until the cheese melts. Salt and pepper to taste and stir in 2 to 3 cups leftover vegetables; I leave the choice and combination to you and your fridge. Pour the vegetables and sauce into a buttered casserole. Now roll out a quick biscuit dough (2 cups Homemade Biscuit Mix (page 82) and 1 cup milk, stir with a fork, knead a couple of times on a floured board, then roll out) and spread it with soft butter. Sprinkle over it 3 or 4 tablespoons chopped parsley (or finely chopped watercress). Roll up, slice in 1-inch slices, and place them around the perimeter of the casserole. Bake 20 minutes at 425° F.

Green and wax beans can serve as the binder in a meat loaf; they take the place of the usual bread crumbs or oatmeal and cut the calorie count. With the price of ground beef going beyond reason, any extender is welcome, almost. Most people still balk at soybean supplements.

Lo-Cal Meat Loaf

Drop into the old blender or the new f.p. bowl (steel blade) ½ cup cooked green and/or wax beans, ½ cup chopped green pepper, 1 small onion, quartered, a splash of Worcestershire sauce, ½ teaspoon each salt, garlic salt, and allspice, and ¼ teaspoon black pepper – also ¼ to ½ cup liquid to keep the blender blades from balking. You can use the sloosh from a ketchup bottle or tomato juice or soup or gravy, whatever comes to hand – but *not* water! Blend these ingredients until they look like wet mud. Place 2 pounds ground beef in a large bowl and punch it in the centre with your fist. This is a very satisfying thing to do and releases all sorts of aggression you didn't know you had. Pour the blender slush into the hole you've punched, take off your rings, and attack the stuff with your bare hands. Knead it together until the mixture is homogenous, and pack it into a 9"×5"×3" loaf pan. Put the pan on a cookie sheet to save your oven from overflow. Bake 1½ hours at 375° F. This is a very wet meat loaf on account of the vegetables. You'll pour off quite a bit of liquid (put it in the dog's dish) before you unmould it on a hot platter to serve. Don't forget to put your rings back on.

Cooked green and/or
 wax beans
Green pepper
Onion
Worcestershire sauce
Salt
Garlic salt
Allspice
Black pepper
Liquid (ketchup, tomato
 juice, soup, gravy, etc.)
Ground beef

You can mix leftover peas with leftover rice but you'll never get away with it if you have kids like mine. They're purists about things like this.

    Corn is a versatile vegetable to cope with in its leftover form because it can be used in baking as well as in vegetable dishes. Our Swedish housekeeper, who handled dough better than she did children, gave me a recipe for corn pudding. It's a delicious way to use up leftover corn in a side dish.

Bergie's Corn Pudding

Sauté 1 medium onion, finely chopped, or 2 or 3 snipped green onions, in 2 tablespoons butter or margarine till soft. Beat 2 eggs with salt and pepper to taste and a pinch of sugar; stir in 1 cup milk and the kernels from 4 or 5 cobs cooked corn (1 to 2 cups corn kernels) or, if you must, the contents of a can of corn, drained, and the onion mixture. Pour into a buttered casserole and top with ½ cup fine bread crumbs; dot with 1 tablespoon butter. Place casserole in water and bake for 45 minutes at 350° F.

Onion or green onions
Butter
Eggs
Salt and pepper
Sugar
Milk
Cooked corn
Bread crumbs

I keep talking about my own biscuit mix, which is cheaper, handier, and more voluminous than any you can buy. It's about to come up again, so you'd better have the basic recipe.

Homemade Biscuit Mix

Flour
Baking powder
Salt
Shortening

Sift together 9 cups flour, 4 tablespoons baking powder, and 2 tablespoons salt into a very large bowl. Cut 2 cups cold shortening into it and proceed to blend that into the flour with a pastry cutter until the mixture looks like cornmeal. That's all. Store it in a tightly covered container on your cupboard shelf. For plain drop biscuits, take 1½ cups mix and ½ cup milk and stir with a fork until moistened. You can also use the mix for dozens of goodies, such as

Corn and Bacon Biscuits

Biscuit mix
Cooked corn
Bacon
Milk

Measure 3 cups Homemade Biscuit Mix into a bowl and drop in ½ to 1 cup or so corn kernels and 4 strips bacon, fried crisp and crumbled. Pour in ¾ cup milk, stir until everything is moistened and adequately introduced, and drop by spoonfuls on an ungreased baking sheet. Bake 12 to 15 minutes at 450° F. Makes a baker's dozen of large biscuits.

The following is more complicated, but well worth the trouble. I call them

Revolving Corn Muffins,

Egg
Buttermilk
Corn oil
Cooked corn
Flour
Baking soda
Cornmeal
Sugar
Baking powder
Salt

because any way you look at them, they're full of corn. Beat 1 egg and stir in 1½ cups buttermilk, ¼ cup corn oil, and ½ to 1 cup leftover corn kernels. Sift together 1½ cups flour, ½ teaspoon baking soda, 1 cup cornmeal, ½ cup sugar, 3 teaspoons baking powder, and 1 teaspoon salt. Pour the wet into the dry ingredients and stir till just moistened; muffins are a disaster if you over-stir. Drop the batter into greased muffin pans and bake 15 to 20 minutes at 450° F. Makes 18 muffins.

Then of course there's succotash and creole. Succotash means you mix your leftover corn with canned or cooked frozen baby lima beans or with leftover lima beans if you're lucky. Put them in the top of a double boiler with some cream and butter, a couple of tablespoons of each, and salt and ground black pepper to taste, and heat it over boiling water until ready to serve. Creole means green and red pepper, tomatoes, and corn, and you're on your own.

I hope mushrooms are a vegetable because that's what I'm about to discuss next. If you don't like mushrooms you can skip this part. Mushrooms are left over whenever you have too many of them. They need not necessarily be cooked. You may have bought mushrooms for an egg-and-mushroom casserole and found you only needed 1 cup when you thought you needed two. Like that. Or you may have discovered a special on mushrooms. I used to have a vegetable man who had specials on mushrooms. I guess he had a damp basement. Anyway, there are lots of little quick things to do with mushrooms, and of course they come in very handy when you're short of meat for a casserole.

A friend of mine served me mushroom salad for lunch a few years ago and I have been addicted ever since. Every time I get a few spare mushrooms (and have no particular goal in mind) they end up in a salad.

Mushroom Salad

Slice beautiful white mushrooms into slender slices, right through the caps and stems, to total 2 cups. Now make a vinaigrette sauce, but with a difference: go easy on the oil for a change because the mushrooms release their own liquid, and go a little heavier on the lemon juice (not vinegar) because that helps keep them white. So – in a small bowl mix together 2 tablespoons salad oil, ¼ cup lemon juice, ½ teaspoon each salt, black pepper, and dry mustard, 1 teaspoon dill weed, 1 tablespoon snipped chives (if you have them), and 2 tablespoons finely chopped parsley. Mix with a fork and pour quickly over the sliced mushrooms. Toss lightly, cover, and refrigerate long enough to allow the flavours to blend and the mushrooms to release liquid. If you have any left over, which I doubt, or if you doubled or tripled the recipe, the salad will keep (covered) in the fridge to serve again the next day. The mushrooms will be darker, but it will be okay.

Raw mushrooms
Salad oil
Lemon juice
Salt
Black pepper
Dry mustard
Dill weed
Chives
Parsley

Mushrooms are very adaptable. They make wonderful companions for a variety of foods. They form a base for many of my compose-a-casseroles and, in fact, have come up in so many different forms in this book already that there is almost nothing I haven't said about them. They go with eggs – in, on top of, and surrounded by. They go into soups, and stews, and spaghetti. They go with artichokes and potatoes and antipasto. Stuffed with blue cheese, they serve as an appetizer. Stuffed with themselves, they make a piquant side dish for roast beef.

Stuffed Mushrooms

Large mushrooms
Salt and pepper
Garlic salt
Parsley
Chives

Carefully remove the stems from very large mushrooms and chop them into a bowl. Now shake in salt, pepper, garlic salt, dill weed, parsley, and chives and mix together. Spoon this mixture into the caps and place them in a shallow baking dish. Heat for 20 minutes in a 300° F. oven to allow the mushrooms to release their own liquid. Interesting note for dieters: this recipe has zilch calories. If you want more calories than that, save the chopped stems for duxelles and fill each mushroom cap with some of your garlic butter (see Garlic Butter). Put the caps in a not-quite-so-shallow baking dish and pour in some heavy cream – enough to cover the bottom of the dish. Bake 25 minutes at 350° F. Very rich. If you have any of these left over after the meal, cut them up and toss them with cooked egg noodles and butter for the next day's lunch.

Duxelles

Mushroom stems
Butter
Salt and pepper
Powdered mushrooms

These are simply chopped mushroom stems sautéed in butter with salt, pepper, and powdered mushrooms added. You can use this stuff in soups and sauces, spaghettis and stews. If you don't have anything going at the moment to put them in, then lift them with a slotted spoon onto little squares of aluminum foil and package them in ¼- or ½-cup amounts. Put the foil packages in a plastic bag, close with a wire twist, and freeze the duxelles until you can think of something to put them in. It'll come to you.

You can also freeze the caps if you ever have a vegetable man like mine and thus a mushroom abundance. Put the caps, unwashed, on a baking sheet or sheets in the freezer; leave until they're frozen, then drop them into plastic bags. To use, dump them in a strainer, wash them under the cold water faucet – this helps thaw them, too – and drop them in your spaghetti sauce pot or some casserole or other.

I don't believe in boiling potatoes for dinner every night. I like more variety in my diet than that and I like potatoes to be thought of as special and treated as such. Knowing that, you will realize that I sometimes have leftover *raw* potatoes as well as leftover cooked – that is, potatoes that have sat too long in the bin and have begun to soften and/or sprout. They, too, must be dealt with. In other days, other gardens, I used to throw the sprouted potatoes into the earth in the spring, and in August we would harvest the most delectable crop of tiny new potatoes that butter ever melted on. Elsie was my mother's helper at the time of my marriage and she taught me more about food than my mother taught me about sex. She gave me a meat grinder for a wedding present. I still keep it in spite of the food processor which has rendered it obsolete (and rusty). Ever heard of a meat grinder as a keep-sake?

I have always done, and still do, make Elsie's potato pancakes.

Elsie's Potato Pancakes

Grate 3 large potatoes and 1 large onion into a bowl. Sprinkle them with salt and black pepper and ⅔ cup flour. Mix and drop a heaping ¼ cup of the mixture onto a hot well-greased griddle (butter or bacon fat) and shape with the back of a spoon into pancake shapes. Brown both sides – quickly, since this helps to hold the pancake together – then lower the heat and cook slowly for 10 or 15 minutes, turning them at least once.

Raw potatoes
Onion
Salt
Black pepper
Flour
Butter or bacon fat

But you can also make potato pancakes that use leftover mashed potatoes, if that's more in your line.

Mashed-Potato Pancakes

Mix 1 cup or so leftover mashed potatoes with 1 egg, beaten, 1 small onion, grated, ½ teaspoon salt, and a generous grind of black pepper. Add milk – enough to moisten the mixture to the point where you can mould and shape it into patties with your hands. Dip the patties in flour and fry them in bacon fat until nicely browned on both sides and good and hot, about 15 minutes.

Mashed potatoes
Egg
Onion
Salt
Black pepper
Milk
Flour
Bacon fat

This next recipe is one of my favourite ways of using up leftover mashed potatoes; in fact, I deliberately plan on having enough left over to make it.

85

Sausage and Potato Casserole

Bulk sausage
Onion slices
Tomato sauce
Mashed potatoes
Butter
Parmesan cheese

Fry 2 pounds bulk sausage meat, cut in slices, until well browned. Lift with a slotted spoon into a large, fairly shallow greased casserole; there should be 1 layer of slices covering the bottom. Top each slice with a thin slice of onion. Pour over the meat and onion a thick tomato sauce – leftover spaghetti sauce is good, or make one from scratch with your frozen tomatoes (see Spanish Sauce). Top with leftover mashed potatoes liberally dotted with butter (1½ tablespoons) and ¼ cup grated Parmesan cheese. Bake 1 hour at 375° F.

You can make any number of meat pies with mashed potato toppings. Why stop at Shepherd's Pie? You can mash a tall can of salmon, undrained, with 1 teaspoon dill weed and 1 cup sour cream and cover it with mashed potatoes dotted with butter. Add 1 teaspoon crushed rosemary to a couple of cups of cubed cooked chicken; gently mix in a can of cream of chicken soup diluted with ⅓ cup milk and top the mixture with butter-dotted mashed potatoes. Or try 1 teaspoon tarragon with leftover beef, sautéed mushrooms, and a bit of gravy or sour cream for moistener, and top that with buttered mashed potatoes. Bake any of these for 45 minutes at 375° F. Here's a more formal recipe for a meat pie.

Meat Pie

Ground beef
Egg
Flour
Garlic salt
Black pepper
Mashed potatoes
Sour cream

Mix 1 pound ground beef with 1 egg, 2 tablespoons flour, 1 teaspoon garlic salt, and ¼ teaspoon black pepper. Press into a 9-inch pie pan. Bake 15 to 20 minutes at 350° F. and then drain off the fat which will have collected. Top with leftover mashed potatoes, frost the potatoes with fork-whipped sour cream, and put back into the oven to heat and brown slightly – about 15 minutes.

I have a feeling pumpkin isn't a vegetable, but I seldom treat it as a fruit so why not include it here? Like corn, pumpkin is extremely adaptable in that it finds its way into baked goods as well as main courses. I have already described what to do with your Hallowe'en pumpkin in the soup chapter; assuming you have a freezer full of Hallowe'en pumpkin, what could be more leftover and available than that? One word of caution. Some years the pumpkin is wetter than others, depending, I suppose, on the amount of rain there has been during the summer. To allow for this, and arrive at an accurate measurement, drain the pumpkin in a strainer before measuring it. Now you're ready to cook.

Pumpkin Bread

Place in your ever-loving blender 2 cups cooked thawed drained pumpkin purée (see page 15), 1½ cups brown sugar, firmly packed, ½ cup salad oil, ½ teaspoon salt, and 3 eggs. Blend well. Sift together 5 cups flour, 2 teaspoons baking powder, 1 teaspoon cinnamon, and ½ teaspoon freshly grated nutmeg into a large bowl. Stir the wet stuff into the dry stuff until the dry stuff isn't dry any more. Pile the batter into 2 buttered loaf pans, 9″×5″×3″ and 8″×4″×2½″ (a big loaf and a small loaf). Bake 1 hour at 325° F.

Cooked pumpkin purée
Brown sugar
Salad oil
Salt
Eggs
Flour
Baking powder
Cinnamon
Nutmeg

The following recipe was given me by my mushroom salad friend, who makes it because she can't make pastry, but it's the lightest, most fetching pumpkin pie you'll find around and not nearly as heavy eating after Thanksgiving dinner as the usual type.

Nancie's Pumpkin Chiffon Pie

Make a graham cracker pie shell: mix 1¼ cups graham cracker crumbs with ¼ cup melted butter, ¼ cup sugar, and ½ teaspoon cinnamon. Press into bottom and side of a 9-inch pie pan, reserving ⅓ cup crumb mixture for topping. Bake 8 minutes at 375° F. Cool and fill. Filling: in the top of a double boiler, beat 3 egg yolks with ½ cup sugar, ½ teaspoon salt, ¼ teaspoon each ground cloves and nutmeg, ½ teaspoon each ginger and cinnamon, 1½ cups pumpkin, canned or home-puréed and drained, and ⅓ cup milk. Cook over boiling water, stirring till thickened. Soak 1 tablespoon gelatin in ¼ cup cold water and then stir into the pumpkin mixture. Beat 3 egg whites with ⅓ cup sugar until stiff but not dry; fold into pumpkin mixture. Pile into the pie shell and sprinkle with reserved crumbs. Chill before serving.

Graham cracker crumbs
Butter
Sugar
Cinnamon
Eggs, separated
Salt
Cloves
Nutmeg
Ginger
Cinnamon
Pumpkin purée
Milk
Gelatin
Water

What about pumpkin as a vegetable? Stick hot pumpkin in halved oranges with the flesh scooped out (save for orange bread), bake them with marshmallows on top and challenge anyone who thinks it's squash.

I like leftover cooked spinach. It's very handy to have around the fridge. One nutritious way of using it up as luncheon for one is to spread it out in a pie pan and slip it under the broiler to heat. Slice 4 ounces of your favourite cheese and spread that over the warm spinach; broil again until the cheese is bubbly. Or you can snip the spinach with your kitchen scissors as it reheats in a little enamel saucepan and use it as a filling for a luncheon omelet. Both meals are quick and full of some vitamin or other. Here's a slightly more elaborate idea for two.

Florentine Quickie

Cooked spinach
Eggs
Cheddar cheese
Salt and pepper

Warm 1 cup cooked spinach, undrained, and arrange in a small buttered casserole or in 2 individual au gratin dishes. Break 4 eggs gently on top of the spinach or two on each individual bed. Sprinkle with grated Cheddar cheese, 1 tablespoon on each egg, and salt and pepper to taste. Bake at 375° F. for 10 to 15 minutes or until the eggs are set.

But maybe you have more spinach than that. It can happen; maybe everyone suddenly had meetings or got sick or went out for dinner. The variables in an average family are endless and unpredictable. What is certain is that you end up with too much of something you'd rather see the last of. Like 2 cups of cooked spinach.

Spinach and Tuna en Coquille

Cooked spinach
Butter
Flour
Light cream
Lemon juice and rind
Salt and pepper
Egg yolk
Tuna

Drain your 2 cups or so of leftover spinach and chop or snip it up with scissors; reheat it in 1 tablespoon butter, tossing it gently now and again. Divide the spinach among 6 scallop shells (or put it in 1 buttered casserole). Make a cream sauce, using 1 tablespoon butter to 1 tablespoon flour and stirring in 1 cup light cream. Add 2 tablespoons lemon juice, 1 teaspoon grated lemon rind, and salt and pepper to taste. Cook and stir until thickened, then stir a little of the sauce into 1 egg yolk so as not to shock it when it meets the whole family. Then stir the integrated egg yolk into the sauce and blend well. Now mix in the contents of 2 drained 7-ounce cans tuna, forked into bite-size chunks. Pour the creamed tuna over the spinach and poke the spinach a bit to let the sauce ooze into it. Bake 45 minutes at 350° F. for the single casserole, 25 to 30 minutes for the scallop shell treatment.

If you have a garden with more than two tomato plants in it, or if you have a neighbour with a garden with more than two tomato plants in it, you will have leftover tomatoes. It is a little-known fact that you *can* freeze tomatoes. Simply wash them and quarter them, cutting out the thick stem end, drop them in a plastic bag, twist it shut with a wire twist, and put it in a waxed carton or in a large plastic bag with the rest of your bagged tomatoes. Freeze. If the tomatoes are tough field tomatoes, you are allowed to peel them before you quarter them. To use, drop them in their frozen state into a saucepan and turn on the heat; meanwhile, assemble the ingredients for a spaghetti or Spanish sauce.

Spaghetti Sauce

Put 2 quarts frozen tomatoes (or two 28-ounce cans if you must) into a saucepan over medium heat and add the sloosh from a ketchup bottle (page 128) if you can spare it. I seem to use a lot of ketchup bottles. Well, try the heel of a can of tomato juice, say about ½ to ¾ cup, and in either case, add a 5½-ounce can tomato paste. Crush in 4 garlic cloves and drop in 1 bay leaf, 1 teaspoon each salt, oregano, and Worcestershire sauce, and ¼ teaspoon black pepper. In a separate frying pan sauté 2 large onions, sliced, in 3 tablespoons oil until soft. If you have any green pepper lying around you can add some thin strips of that too. Put the vegetables in the tomato saucepan and brown a pound of ground beef in the remaining onion-oil, breaking it up with a wooden spoon and cooking it until the meat loses all its pink colour. Add drained meat to tomato sauce. If you have any mushrooms, canned, left-over, whatever, drop them into the sauce. If you're using fresh ones, add them later, so as not to discourage them too much. A heel of a bottle of red wine would be nice, so nice in fact, that if you don't have any, why not splash in ¼ cup sherry? Taste the sauce and adjust the seasoning, turn the heat down to low, cover the pot, and leave it alone for at least an hour. It's best to make this a day ahead of time to give it a chance to ripen. Not only that – when the sauce is chilled, the fat congeals on the surface and can easily be lifted off. Reheat the sauce the next day while you boil your spaghetti or vermicelli. Don't forget to remove the bay leaf! Of course, the sauce can be frozen and used a lot later. At the end of your spaghetti meal, mix all your leftover pasta with all the leftover sauce, and put it in a casserole. Freeze it for a later spaghetti casserole. When you're ready for spaghetti again, thaw it,

Frozen or canned
  tomatoes
Ketchup or tomato juice
  and tomato paste
Garlic
Bay leaf
Salt
Oregano
Worcestershire sauce
Black pepper
Onions
Oil
Green pepper
Ground beef
Mushrooms
Red wine

sprinkle ½ cup grated Parmesan cheese on top, and bake it for 45 minutes to 1 hour at 350° F.

Spanish Sauce is Spanish Rice without the rice.

Spanish Sauce

Green pepper	Sauté 1 large green pepper, cut in strips, and 3 large onions, sliced, in 6 tablespoons salad oil until the vegetables are tender. Add 2 quarts frozen tomatoes, a 7½-ounce can tomato sauce, 1 bay leaf, 2 teaspoons salt, and ½ teaspoon freshly ground black pepper. That's the basic, which you cook over low heat for an hour. But if you're feeling very olé, you can shake in some red pepper flakes, anything from 1 teaspoon to 1 tablespoon if you're feeling wild. And 1 teaspoon cumin seed, crushed, does wonderful things, with or without the red pepper. Go ahead and experiment; they're your tomatoes. If you want to use this in the Sausage and Potato Casserole (page 86), blend it in the blender first to make 2 quarts of very smooth tomato sauce.
Onions	
Salad oil	
Tomatoes	
Tomato sauce	
Bay leaf	
Salt	
Black pepper	
Red pepper flakes	
Cumin seed	

You don't have to keep making sauces even though you're loaded with tomatoes. A plethora of tomatoes can be dealt with in other ways.

Tomatoes with Sour Cream

Tomatoes	Slice 6 ripe tomatoes in inch-thick slices and dip both sides in a mixture of ½ cup flour, 1 teaspoon sugar, and a sprinkling of salt and pepper. Sauté the tomatoes quickly but gently in 4 tablespoons butter or margarine, turning to brown both sides evenly. Then, still quickly and gently, stir in 1 cup sour cream. Cook just enough to heat but not long enough to curdle it. Serve at once.
Flour	
Sugar	
Salt and pepper	
Butter	
Sour cream	

For those of you who live in a northern climate, as I do, you know you must take the last tomatoes off the plants while they are still green to beat the frost. For the next couple of weeks you clutter up your kitchen with tomatoes – wrapped in newspaper, since you're encouraging them to ripen and redden off the vine. Rejoice! You can do lovely things with green tomatoes and unclutter your kitchen.

90

Curried Green Tomatoes

Melt 2 tablespoons butter in a frying pan and stir in 1 teaspoon curry powder, heating to release the full power of the curry. Now gently sauté in the curry-butter 2 cups sliced green tomatoes, turning as necessary, until they are tender. Salt and pepper to taste. Delicious.

Butter
Curry powder
Green tomatoes
Salt and pepper

And green tomato mincemeat is so good that if I don't have any leftover green tomatoes, I go looking for them. They're not always easy to buy. You have to find someone with a cluttered kitchen who doesn't know what she's missing.

Green Tomato Mincemeat

Take a really big saucepan and brace yourself for sore hands from all the chopping. Drop into it 6 cups chopped apples, 6 cups chopped green tomatoes, 4 cups brown sugar, firmly packed, and 3 cups raisins. Mix together 1 teaspoon each cinnamon and cloves, and ¾ teaspoon each allspice, mace, and white pepper, and drop into the pan. Add 2 tablespoons salt and ¼ cup white vinegar. Stir well, bring to a boil, cover, and simmer for 3 hours, stirring occasionally. Remove from heat and stir in ¾ cup butter and ¼ cup brandy; cool. Pack in freezer containers and freeze. Keeps indefinitely – well, up to 2 years. Use for pies, tarts, cookies, and breads. Some years this is wetter than others. If it strikes you as being too wet, lift it into the freezer cartons with a slotted spoon. Don't throw away that spicy brandy juice, though. Use it for an ice cream sauce.

Apples
Green tomatoes
Brown sugar
Raisins
Cinnamon
Cloves
Allspice
Mace
White pepper
Salt
White vinegar
Butter
Brandy

As you know very well, a stock pot is a perfect haven for your poor, tired vegetables, whether raw and limp or cooked and left over. But sometimes, people have missed a meal or two and some perfectly good veg are lying there waiting to be used. Consider the lesson that ratatouille teaches us – namely, that a lot of different vegetables get along very well together and are, in fact, greater than the sum of their parts. Take a lesson from the peasants who invented the dish and invent your own. In doing so, you are helping not only your family, which needs the vitamins, but your fridge, which is tired.

91

Ratatouille

Mushrooms
Green pepper
Celery
Tomatoes
Eggplant
Green onions
Zucchini
Onion
Butter
Garlic
Salt and pepper

Take stock of your refrigerator. A few mushrooms, half a green pepper, 2 or 3 limp stalks of celery (not *too* limp), 1 or 2 tired tomatoes, part of a darkening eggplant from one that was too big to cook all of the first time, a couple of tattered green onions, and 2 or 3 unassuming zucchini. It really doesn't matter. Melt 1 tablespoon butter in a pot; cut a zingy new onion into small dice and toss it in to act as master of ceremonies. Trim and slice everything else into the pot. Crush in 1 clove garlic, salt and pepper lightly, mix gently, and turn on the heat: high to get it started, then medium-low. If you don't like the results after a scant 15 minutes, you like your vegetables overdone. If you don't like it anyway, then you are still a child at heart and I give up on your ever liking vegetables.

Chapter 6

Rice, Beans, Pasta, Cereals: Waist Not, Want Not

"It must be nice to run a boardinghouse and not have to worry about something different for dinner every day," said the American humourist Kin Hubbard. Your family may feel as if you *are* running a boardinghouse if you have much to do with rice because rice can rapidly get ahead of one. I will never forget the disaster that befell a friend of mine who, when making her first paella, decided to triple the rice called for in the recipe. She almost ran out of containers. She was having company for dinner and in addition to two helpings, each of the female guests had to take a casserole of the stuff away with her. Because of that memory it was years before I attempted my first paella. The same thing could happen with Hopping John if one failed to exercise restraint. I think this southern beans and rice combination may have acquired its intriguing name from an erosion of the phrase *au pension* — at the boardinghouse. Where else would such a hearty and inexpensive means of using up beans and rice have originated?

Hopping John

Soak overnight 1 pound dried beans (white, pinto, or any type that appeals to you) in cold water to cover. In the morning add more water if necessary to cover the beans, and 1 onion, quartered, and 1 teaspoon salt. Boil gently until tender. Beans vary. You have to test them: pick up a few in a spoon and blow on them gently. If the skins pop, they're done. You can also chew one. You don't want your beans *al dente*. When the beans are cooked, combine

Dried beans
Water
Onion
Salt
Cooked rice
Cooked ham
Chicken stock

93

them in a large soup pot or Dutch oven with about 2 cups leftover cooked rice; simmer them slowly until they have a chance to blend their flavours. Bits of leftover chopped ham may be added to the bean-rice mixture and any interesting dollops of leftover sauces or a little chicken stock if the mixture seems dry. Beans and rice can absorb a lot of moisture. The amounts specified here are generous enough to serve to a small boardinghouse crowd or an after-ski party – along with a large baked ham or fried country sausage and interesting bread.

Years ago, carried away by a television cooking hostess who suggested that it would be a good idea to have a quart of cooked rice in the fridge at all times, I cooked a mess of rice and put it in the fridge. Two days later, fifteen minutes before guests were due to arrive for dinner, I discovered that a faulty recipe had neglected to tell me to precook the rice in a seafood-and-rice casserole; there were hard, white kernels swimming in the shrimp and tomato sauce. Aha, I thought, I just happen to have some cooked rice on hand. I strained the sauce, picked out the shrimp, peppers, etc., added my rice and put the casserole back in the oven to recover. No one but me knew. You'd think after an experience like that I'd always have cooked rice around, but no. Now I read recipes carefully. Here is a base for almost anything, using leftover cooked rice and anything else you happen to have left over.

Basic Compose-a-Casserole

Butter	Melt ½ cup butter and stir in ½ cup flour until blended. Stir in 3 cups milk and cook and stir until the sauce is thick. Season with salt and pepper. Now look around. A bit of red or green pepper, chopped, is nice. If you have a few stalks of celery too tired to serve for nibbling but too snappy for soup, dice them in too, along with some snipped green onions, tops and bottoms. Any odds and ends of cheese can be grated and added, and my faithful friend the mushroom would not be out of place. Stir everything until the cheese melts and is blended in. Now stir in the leftover cooked rice, 1 or 2 cups, and 2 cups, more or less, leftover cubed cooked meat – turkey or lamb or chicken – or open 2 small, 7-ounce cans salmon or tuna. Turn into a medium-sized (1½-quart) casserole and top with more grated cheese. Bake at 400° F. for 30 to 40 minutes.
Flour	
Milk	
Salt and pepper	
Red or green pepper	
Celery	
Green onions	
Cheese	
Mushrooms	
Cooked rice	
Cooked meat or canned fish	

More formal is a composition which I call

Chicken and Rice

Sauté 1 small onion, chopped, and ¼ cup chopped green pepper in 4 tablespoons butter or margarine till soft. Sprinkle over this ½ cup flour; stir till flour is blended in. Stir in ½ cup light cream and 1½ cups chicken stock; cook, stirring, over medium heat until the sauce thickens. Add 1 teaspoon Worcestershire sauce, ¼ cup dry sherry, 1 pimiento, chopped, and 1 cup sliced mushrooms. You may substitute 1 can mushroom stems and pieces, drained, substituting the mushroom liquid from the can for part of the stock if your fridge does not yield fresh mushrooms at the drop of an improvisation. Now adjust the seasoning and introduce a little sauce to 1 egg yolk. Stir the egg and sauce back into the main body and blend it in. Now fold in 1 cup cooked rice and 1½ to 2½ cups cut-up cooked chicken. Turn the mixture gently into an oven-to-table casserole, top with buttered bread crumbs mixed with grated Parmesan cheese (½ cup total), and bake 30 minutes at 350° F. If this is to be refrigerated and cooked later, increase the cooking time to 45 minutes.	Onion Green pepper Butter Flour Light cream Chicken stock Worcestershire sauce Dry sherry Pimiento Mushrooms Egg yolk Cooked rice Cooked chicken Bread crumbs Parmesan cheese

While we're still messing about with the cream sauce, try this with the rice the next time you decide not to make rice croquettes:

Rice Rolls

Stir about 1 cup cream sauce into 1 cup cooked rice to get a heavy, almost spreadable, consistency. If you like, you can add some bits of grated cheese or some chopped mushrooms or pimientos, but your object is a thick paste. Now splot about a tablespoon of this mixture on a packaged ham slice (they come out thinner and less holey than I can ever slice ham at home), ooze it out to the edges, and roll up the ham slice around the rice, securing with a wooden toothpick. You might fill about 16 ham slices this way, depending on how generous you are with the rice filling. Lay the rolls in individual squares of aluminum foil and seal each in turn into a little package, removing the toothpicks as you go along. Place the foil rolls in a baking dish and heat them gently at 325° F. for 35	Cream sauce
	Cooked rice
	Grated cheese, chopped
	  mushrooms or
	  pimientos
	Ham slices

minutes. These make a pleasant luncheon dish or a surprise nibbler with evening coffee for guests.

Some years ago *Gourmet* magazine had a series of articles on Frozen Assets and Dividend Cooking. As a busy mother of very small children at the time, I leapt at the chance of cooking ahead and resting later, and so I tried most of the recipes. One in particular, involving rice, seemed to provide our little family with more rice than we could cope with—even with the help of a forgetful freezer. That whole winter, at suitably decent intervals, I kept drawing out another package of the everlasting stuff until one evening my oldest daughter, then six, came out to the kitchen to see what was on the menu, and when confronted with this, exclaimed (as many would doubt they would ever hear a six-year-old exclaim), "Oh no! Not Armenian Rice Pilaf again!" Here is Elaine Ross' recipe for that recurrent delicacy—but reduced in quantity so that you may see an end of it.

Armenian Pilaf

Fine noodles
Pine nuts
Butter
Rice
Currants
Chicken stock
Salt
Allspice
Black pepper
Parsley

Sauté 1 cup fine noodles and ⅓ cup pine nuts in ¼ cup melted butter, stirring until the nuts are golden. Add 1½ cups raw rice and 1 tablespoon currants; cook and stir for 5 minutes. Add 3 cups boiling chicken stock, 1 teaspoon salt, ½ teaspoon allspice, and ⅛ teaspoon black pepper. Simmer the pilaf for 20 minutes or until the rice is tender. Stir with a fork, remove from heat, and let stand, covered, for 10 minutes. Serve sprinkled with chopped parsley.

I'm not really a fan of Spanish Rice because when I was first married I bought a can of it and found the contents to be tomato sauce with *one* grain of rice. Obviously it was the last can on the production line. It's incidents like this that force us to become cooks. My problem as a cook is I don't know when to stop. There are always so many mouths to feed, and the spectre of that single grain of rice haunts me. So, though I will give you a simple recipe for Spanish Rice, bear in mind that, given my head, I would add browned ground beef, a can of corn niblets, maybe some leftover garlic sausage, cut up, or some chopped bologna slices, a few lonely mushrooms, and maybe even some sliced black olives. Stop me!

Spanish Rice

Sauté 1 medium onion, chopped, 2 cloves garlic, sliced, and 1 green pepper, chopped, in 2 tablespoons oil until the onions are soft and yellow. Stir in a 20-ounce can tomatoes, liquid and all (or a quart box of home-frozen tomatoes – see page 89), and 1 cup or more cooked rice. Stir in ¼ teaspoon paprika, ½ teaspoon chili powder, 1 teaspoon salt, and ¼ teaspoon black pepper. Simmer until the ingredients become friendly; serve as a main dish for lunch or as a side dish for dinner with something else – the something else is your problem.

Onion
Garlic
Green pepper
Oil
Tomatoes
Cooked rice
Paprika
Chili powder
Salt
Black pepper

Chinese fried rice uses precooked rice as its base and provides another excellent vehicle for nuggets of leftover meat and perhaps some interesting vegetables as well. I like to use this method with leftover tongue. Cold or hot, sliced tongue is a joy until one gets to the root of the matter and then no matter how you slice it, it's a mess. Still good but not very neat. Better to chop it up and put it into.

Tongue Fried Rice

Sauté 6 slices bacon until almost crisp; remove from pan and drain, setting aside 2 slices. Cut all the slices into little pieces, but keep the 2 slices' worth in a separate pile from the remaining 4 slices. Stir 2 cups cooked rice into the hot bacon fat; toss until the rice is well coated. Beat 1 egg with 2 tablespoons Japanese soy sauce; stir into the rice. Add 2 cups cubed cooked tongue (you are allowed to use pork or chicken if you prefer), and ¾ cup sliced mushrooms. Leftover peas or a little chopped green pepper or pimiento may be added too, if desired (that means: if they're sitting there in the refrigerator not doing anything). Stir in the 4 cut-up slices of bacon and then adjust the seasoning. Sprinkle the remaining 2 strips' worth on top, cover the pan, heat gently for 15 minutes, and serve. This is best done in a wok.

Bacon
Cooked rice
Egg
Soy sauce
Cooked tongue (or pork or chicken)
Mushrooms
Cooked peas, or green pepper or pimiento

For a real quickie with leftover rice, though – and this is one of the children's favourites – pretend you're making an instant mix. Put 2 tablespoons oil in a wok or frying pan and heat it. Stir into the oil 2 tablespoons instant chicken soup and 2 tablespoons each instant onion and dried parsley. Mix the seasonings for a moment, then add 1 to 2 cups cooked rice. Stir to coat it with the seasonings and oil, reduce the heat, cover, and allow to heat through. If you want it fairly crisp, keep the heat high and keep stirring. Instant fried rice!

Leftover rice need not be served hot. Cold, it provides a *raison d'être* for any number of cooked vegetables which you may feel are not earning their keep in the refrigerator.

Rice Salad

Cooked rice
Cooked green and wax
 beans
Cooked lima beans or
 peas
Spanish onion
Green pepper
French dressing
Dill weed

Combine 2 cups, more or less, cold cooked rice with 1 cup each cold cooked green and wax beans (both kinds cut rather than Frenched), plus 1 cup cold cooked baby lima beans or green peas. Slice 1 Spanish onion and 1 green pepper into thin rings and add to the rice-vegetable mixture. Toss lightly with about ½ cup French dressing, sprinkle generously with dried dill weed, and toss again. Cover and refrigerate for at least 2 hours before serving to allow the inmates to adjust to each other. This amount will serve more than six people, but I am assuming that if you are using leftovers, in no case will you have the full or exact amount specified. It doesn't matter.

The prime rule of a leftover cook is: improvise. "A host is like a general," said the Latin poet Horace. "It takes a mishap to reveal his genius." The same is true of a leftover cook. Happy accidents and inspired substitutions can have delectable results. Be prepared to use anything that comes to hand, but also be sure to have on hand what you want to be prepared with.

There are other ways to use up rice besides throwing it in soup.

Rice Waffles

Eggs
Corn oil
Buttermilk
Sifted flour
Baking powder
Baking soda
Salt
Cooked rice

Drop in the blender container 2 eggs, ⅓ cup corn oil, 2 cups buttermilk, 2 cups sifted flour, 2 teaspoons baking powder, ½ teaspoon baking soda, and ½ teaspoon salt. Blend for 20 seconds and turn into a bowl. Stir in 1 cup cooked rice – gently (so as not to mash the rice) but thoroughly. Bake in a waffle iron.

Rice Cakes

Put in container of blender or food processor bowl 1 egg, ½ cup milk, 1 tablespoon oil, ½ small green pepper, ¼ onion, both cut up, ½ teaspoon salt, and 2 cups cooked rice. Blend. Dump into a bowl and stir in ½ cup flour and 4 strips bacon, cooked until crisp, then crumbled. Cook in butter or margarine in a skillet, dropping the mixture by tablespoonfulls (tablespoons-full?) into the hot fat, browning and turning once. Keep warm in the oven until all are cooked. Layer them between sheets of paper towelling so they don't get soggy.

Egg
Milk
Oil
Green pepper
Onion
Salt
Cooked rice
Flour
Bacon
Butter

Rice Muffins

Drop in blender or f.p. bowl 1 cup milk, 2 eggs, 5 tablespoons corn oil, and 1 cup cooked rice. Blend; plop into bowl into which has been sifted 1½ cups flour, ½ cup sugar (unless the rice has been cooked in a salty stock, in which case make it 2 tablespoons sugar. Why fight it?), ¼ teaspoon salt, and 3 teaspoons baking powder. Stir to moisten all the dry ingredients and bake in muffin pans 25 minutes at 400° F. Makes 1 dozen muffins.

Milk
Eggs
Corn oil
Cooked rice
Flour
Sugar
Salt
Baking powder

Even a little rice can go a long way. A few tablespoons of cooked rice need not be thrown out. Drop them thoughtfully into your soup du jour and then you can call it Something and Rice Soup. Stir a few tablespoons of rice into ½ pound well-seasoned ground beef, and roll the mixture up into cabbage rolls; bake in a tomato sauce for an hour or so in a 325° F. oven and call it Almost Instant Holopchi. Or add to the cooked rice 2 tablespoons pine nuts sautéed in olive oil, 2 tablespoons currants, 1 tablespoon tomato paste, and 1 teaspoon dried mint leaves. Drop the mixture by teaspoonfuls on grape leaves, then roll them up. Put the cigar-shaped rolls into a casserole, dribble them with olive oil, and bake an hour at 325° F. Serve cold or lukewarm as an hors d'oeuvre called Dolmathes.

Pasta is like rice; it's nice to have around the fridge. It's a good mixer, gets along well with other ingredients, and offers a platform for presentation of small amounts of disparate foods which, without macaroni, might never meet. It's gorgeous in a salad.

Macaroni Salad

Mayonnaise
Sour cream
Horseradish
Salt and pepper
Cooked elbow macaroni
Celery
Green and red pepper
Parsley
Hard-cooked eggs

Mix ½ cup each mayonnaise and sour cream with 2 tablespoons prepared horseradish, and salt and pepper to taste. Put 2 cups cold cooked elbow macaroni in a salad bowl with 1 cup chopped celery, 1 green pepper and 1 red pepper, chopped, and toss thoroughly with the dressing. Gently stir in ½ cup chopped fresh parsley and 3 hard-cooked eggs, chopped. Refrigerate at least 1 hour before serving – preferably 3 hours. Garnish with quartered tomatoes, hard-cooked eggs, and snippets of fresh watercress or parsley.

Sometimes in making up a family casserole which calls for egg noodles, one finds that a whole package of noodles is more than the recipe calls for, but that small amount remaining is not worth keeping on the shelf. The small amount suddenly looks quite large when cooked and wet. Oh well, cook the whole package anyway and do this with the leftover noodles.

Noodle Pud

Cooked noodles
Egg
Sour cream
Salt and pepper
Cottage cheese
Cheddar cheese
Bread or cracker crumbs
Butter
Mushrooms or bacon

Press 2 cups (or so) well-drained medium or large egg noodles into an 11½"×9"×2" baking pan. Beat an egg with ¾ cup sour cream and salt and pepper to taste; pour the mixture over the noodles. Press over the noodles whatever you have left of a carton of cottage cheese, about 1 cup (make up the difference with sour cream or yogurt if you don't have enough). Bake, uncovered, for 30 minutes at 350° F. Remove from oven and sprinkle the pud. generously, that is, *load it*, with ½ cup shredded Cheddar cheese mixed with ½ cup bread or cracker crumbs. Dot with 1½ tablespoons soft butter. This would be nice topped with mushroom caps placed in strategic and attractive positions, but you know your fridge better than I do. Failing mushrooms, what about partially cooked bacon slices? Anyway, put the casserole back in the oven and bake for another 15 minutes or until the cheese is browned.

Dried beans are beautiful. I find it difficult ever to think of beans as leftovers, but then that's true of rice and pasta as well. *They* are never left over; other things are. Beans are so long and lovingly cooked they're like friends of the family by the time you're through with them. One or two wieners can be cut up and added to your beans, whether you have made old-fashioned baked beans, or Hopping John (page 93), or have a few extra kidney beans around from an overly ambitious chili con carne (and belong to the meat-separate-from-the-beans school of chili). So can Italian or garlic sausage or chorizo (though that's better with leftover chick peas). You can make a bastard minestrone by dumping the last handful of beans into your current soup, along with whatever other interesting vegetables survived last night's dinner. Do as the Mexicans do and cope with your beans by frying them. They're called Refried Beans even though they weren't fried the first time.

Refried Beans

Mash 2 cups cooked kidney beans with 1 clove garlic, crushed. Sauté 1 onion, chopped, in 2 tablespoons salad oil; add the mashed beans. Heat over low heat, stirring to prevent the beans from sticking to the pan. Stir in ½ cup grated Cheddar cheese and heat until the cheese has melted. Serve beans topped with more grated cheese and shredded lettuce. Lunch for four.

Cooked kidney beans
Garlic
Onion
Salad oil
Cheddar cheese
Shredded lettuce

If you ever cook cornmeal mush or oatmeal, you will inevitably face leftover quantities of these cereals.

Fried Cornmeal Mush

Pack whatever is left of your cornmeal-for-breakfast into a greased loaf pan; refrigerate. The next morning turn out the loaf and slice it into ½-inch-thick slices. Dip the slices in flour and fry them in butter, turning as you please, until they are heated through and browned nicely on both sides. Serve with butter and maple syrup and slices of fried bacon.

Cornmeal mush
Flour
Butter

Oatmeal Bread

Drop 1 package dry yeast into ¼ cup warm water in the blender container or food processor bowl (steel blade), and allow to stand for 5 minutes. Blend. Add ⅓ cup brown sugar, 1 tablespoon corn oil, and 1½ cups leftover cooked oatmeal, lukewarm. Blend again and turn into a mixing bowl. Stir at first, then knead in, 3 to 3½ cups flour. The dough is heavy and quite sticky. Place in greased

Yeast
Warm water
Brown sugar
Corn oil
Cooked oatmeal
Flour

101

bowl, cover, and let rise in a warm place for 1½ hours. Shape into a loaf and place in greased loaf pan, 9″×5″×3″, cover, and let rise again 1 hour. Bake 40 minutes at 375° F.

I have one friend who wouldn't give me a thank-you for a recipe like that because her family prefers old cooked oatmeal (some like it in the pot nine days old). There's no accounting for tastes, least of all in breakfast, which is, to say the least, a very intimate meal. Maybe that's why most homemakers run the breakfast hour like a boardinghouse. It's safer that way.

Chapter 7

Fruit: Never Underestimate the Power of a Marshmallow

It was Brillat-Savarin who said, "Tell me what you eat and I'll tell you what you are." I wonder what he would have said about people who eat marshmallows. Actually, this chapter is about fruit, but when it comes to fruit, marshmallows come in awfully handy.

There is a popular thing that people around here keep bringing to potluck suppers and nobody ever knows whether to serve it with the main course or to bring it on as dessert – so they do both because there are usually two or three bowls of the stuff.

Ambrosia

It's as good a way as any to use up coconut and other fruits. Drop 1½ cups mini-marshmallows or cut-up whole ones into a large bowl. Now add 1 or 2 cut-up oranges (or 1 can mandarin oranges, drained, if you're not worried about tired oranges), 1 can pineapple chunks, drained, and/or 1 can fruit cocktail, drained. You can substitute other fruit: maybe a peach or a pear you want to use before it goes soft, or one last serving of same, canned, which is cluttering up the fridge. One banana can also find its way in here, as can a few cantaloupe balls or some green grapes. Add ½ cup shredded coconut and a few halved maraschino cher-

Marshmallows
Oranges
Pineapple chunks and/or
 fruit cocktail
Banana
Cantaloupe
Green grapes
Coconut
Maraschino cherries
Sour cream

103

ries for zip and dash – also colour. Now toss the whole thing – gently, gently – with sour cream, starting with ½ cup and working your way up to a cup, depending on how much fruit you have used. Refrigerate at least 4 hours before serving to allow the flavours to mingle. Never, as I say, underestimate the power of a marshmallow.

Actually, I don't like food like this. It's too sweet and yecchy. But lots of people do. I have one friend who happens to be a male chauvinist who has developed a whole theory of male and female food. This Ambrosia, he maintains, is the kind of thing women serve on lettuce leaves at a bridge party. I don't like bridge, either.

I feel about baked apples the way I do about creamed celery: I hate them. And since it's my cookbook, I don't have to talk about them. But applesauce is another matter. Kate is the only one in the family who does not like applesauce, an interesting foible that I respect. Applesauce is a great thing to be able to do to leftover apples, that is, apples that have microscopic blemishes on them which render them unfit for fastidious children like mine to eat. Most people put cinnamon in their applesauce; some people put nutmeg; I have known some who prefer it seasoned with ground cloves. When I get them, mostly in little packets at Hallowe'en, or by the pound at the Valentine season, I drop into the cooked apples a handful of cinnamon hearts. They serve a threefold purpose: they sweeten, they season, and they colour the applesauce pink. Here's something you can do with applesauce, if you haven't sweetened it and maybe even if you have.

Apple Cake

Flour	Sift together 2½ cups flour, 1½ cups sugar, 3 teaspoons baking
Sugar	powder, 1 teaspoon baking soda, 1 teaspoon salt, and ½ teaspoon
Baking powder	cinnamon. Pour in all at once ½ cup salad oil and ½ cup butter-
Baking soda	milk, 1 cup thick applesauce, unsweetened, and 1 egg. If you had
Salt	already sweetened the applesauce before you decided to make this
Cinnamon	cake, then reduce the sugar to 1 to 1¼ cups, depending on how
Salad oil	sweet you made your applesauce in the first place. Beat well for 2
Buttermilk	minutes on medium speed of the electric mixer until the ingredi-
Applesauce	ents are well blended and smooth. Pour the batter into a
Egg	10½″ × 8½″ pan and bake 40 to 45 minutes in a 350° F. oven. You
	can frost this right in the pan, with a vanilla butter frosting.

When daughter Kate started cooking she had, of course, her own cookbook to work from and one recipe in it was her favourite – oatmeal cookies. One day when she made them something went wrong and they wouldn't metamorphose into cookies, but instead remained stubbornly disparate. Bad enough when disaster overtakes us grown-ups in the kitchen, but what trauma for a little one! This is when the hard facts of life begin to emerge, when one is truly aware of some malevolent force in the universe, when despite all one's best efforts, jelly refuses to jell, sauce lumpishly refuses to smooth, fudge refuses to harden (as the muscles of the beating arm knot with pain), and cookies, what were meant to be cookies, crumble at the touch of a finger. In rush apples and mother to the rescue.

Apple Crips

It's really crisp, but all the kids called it crips when they were little and I like the sound. Peel, core, and slice 6 to 8 apples – but if you have 10 apples you want to use up, I don't mind. Mix together 3 tablespoons sugar and 1 teaspoon cinnamon and toss it gently through the apples. Spread the apples out in a buttered baking dish, 9-inch square for fewer apples, a larger size if you used more. In a small bowl, mix with a fork ¾ cup brown sugar, packed, 4 tablespoons flour, ½ cup quick-cooking oatmeal, ¼ teaspoon salt, and ½ cup salad oil, until the mixture is uniformly damp and crumbly. Sprinkle the mixture over the apples and then lift them slightly to allow the crumblies to get cozy. Dot with butter – a total of 1½ tablespoons – and pop into a 375° F. oven for 45 minutes. Serve warm, with ice cream or whipped cream. That's the basic recipe. It's even better with Kate's Oatmeal Crumbs mixed in with it. If you have a disaster of a crumbly cookie like that, substitute it for the flour-oatmeal mixture. That's how stars are born. And a while back when we were considering Sour Cream Coffee Cake (page 60) I said you might get caught with more filling than you needed. Make the basic apple crips, but sprinkle over it any leftover brown-sugar-pecan filling that you have thoughtfully saved in a screwtop jar.

Apples
Sugar
Cinnamon
Brown sugar
Flour
Quick-cooking oatmeal
Salt
Salad oil
Butter

If you have only 2 suspicious-looking apples, obviously you won't make applesauce or crips, but you can make a delicious apple bread.

Apple Bread

Flour
Baking soda
Baking powder
Salt
Cinnamon
Ground cloves
Lemon juice
Apples
Salad oil
Orange juice
Eggs
Sugar
Walnuts (optional)

Sift into a large bowl 3 cups flour, 1 teaspoon baking soda, 1½ teaspoons baking powder, 1 teaspoon salt, ½ teaspoon cinnamon, and ¼ teaspoon ground cloves. Pour ⅓ cup lemon juice into your blender container or f.p. bowl (steel blade) and drop in 2 apples, peeled, cored, and sliced. Blend until the apples are sloshy, then add ½ cup salad oil, ½ cup orange juice, 2 eggs, and 1¾ cups sugar. Blend again. If you want, you can blend in 1 cup walnuts, but this is optional. Stir the wet ingredients into the dry ingredients until the dry aren't anymore and pour the batter into 2 buttered loaf pans, one 9″×5″×3″ and one 8″×4×2½″. Bake in a 350° F. oven for 1 hour and 15 minutes. Cool on a rack before slicing. Use the smaller bread for a child's tea party or a neighbour's treat.

If you have only one apple, peel it and grate it into your favourite pancake batter and hope no one will notice it. You can also hide it in teeny slices in a bread pudding. If anyone says, "Hey, who put apples in the bread pudding?" say: "Aha! You noticed! You win first prize!" and give him or her a wishbone or a band-aid or something.

My mother's father ran a general store and used to take the unsaleable perishable items home for the family to use. It trained my mother to enjoy *really* ripe fruit, and certainly I tolerate it very well. Not my kids. Infinitesimal specks on bananas relegate the offending fruit to the bottom of the fruit basket. I sometimes think, however, that the children leave bananas lying around on purpose so that I'll be forced to bake something with them. There's no doubt that baked things with bananas in them are good, although Liz doesn't like banana cake or bread. The moral is that you can't please all of my family all of the time. How about yours?

Did you know you can freeze bananas? The idea came as a shock to me, being of the generation that grew up with the Chiquita Banana hit song which reminded us never, never, never to put bananas in the refrigerator. But if you have mushy bananas and no time to bake them into something or not enough of them to do anything else with, simply peel them and mash them with a fork into that sludge they form, pack them into a plastic container with a tight-fitting lid, and freeze them. Thaw later and bake in something.

106

Banana Bars

Sift together ¾ cup flour, 1 teaspoon baking powder, and ⅛ teaspoon salt. Combine ¼ cup salad oil with 1 cup brown sugar, firmly packed; stir in 1 egg, beaten. Stir this mixture into the dry ingredients and add ⅔ cup or so mashed bananas and ½ cup chopped nuts. It doesn't matter if you have ¾ cup banana mush, but try not to have less than ½ cup. Two bananas will do it. Mix all the ingredients well – say 2 minutes at medium speed on the electric mixer if you don't mind dirtying it. Pour the batter in to a buttered 8-inch square pan. Bake 35 to 40 minutes in a 350° F. oven.

Flour
Baking powder
Salt
Salad oil
Brown sugar
Egg
Mashed bananas
Chopped nuts

Banana Muffins

Sift into your bowl 2 cups flour, 2 teaspoons baking powder, ½ teaspoon baking soda, and ¾ teaspoon salt. In the blender or the food processor bowl (steel blade), blend 2 or 3 bananas with 1 teapoon lemon juice, then add 1 egg, ½ cup salad oil, ¼ cup strong black coffee or – more fun – rum, and ½ cup brown sugar, packed. Blend till well mixed, then stir this mixture quickly and lightly into the dry ingredients. They say you should never stir muffins more than 25 strokes and I believe them. Horrible things happen to muffins if you overstir. Fill greased muffin pans ⅔ full and press half a pecan into each batter-filled cup. Bake for 20 minutes in a 400° F. oven.

Flour
Baking powder
Baking soda
Salt
Bananas
Lemon juice
Egg
Salad oil
Coffee or rum
Brown sugar
Pecans

If the bananas are too dark for your picayune children, but not really mushy enough to warrant the effort of bread or muffins, make a pudding or pie. If you happen to have a baked pie shell lying around (sometimes I do), slice the offending bananas into it in a pleasing, overlapping, ever-widening circle and pour over it a quick cook-and-stir vanilla pudding. Top with whipped cream.

A mushy banana can gain a whole new self-image in a nog, with egg and milk and sugar (and rum?) and you don't need a food processor to reassure it. One soft, sad banana can also be immensely comforted by the addition of a couple of scoops of ice cream, with a strawberry jam topping or any syrups or sweet sauces you may find gumming up your fridge. That is, if you have anyone young enough and thin enough to eat it. Otherwise, whip it up to glory in a frosting and spread the bounty and the calories around.

Banana Frosting

Cream
Butter
Cocoa
Coffee
Banana
Icing sugar

In the small bowl of your mixer put 2 tablespoons cream, 3 tablespoons butter, 3 tablespoons cocoa, dry, 1 tablespoon liquid coffee, and 1 banana, mashed. Sift in 1 cup icing sugar and then turn on the beaters. Beat like mad, adding sugar until you have the desired frosting consistency. This will frost more than 1 cake, but it keeps very nicely in the fridge until another naked cake comes along.

Banana Cake

Bananas
Butter
Sugar
Eggs
Flour
Baking powder
Salt
Sour cream
Baking soda

Actually I prefer banana frosting on a chocolate or a vanilla cake so don't think I'm trying to start something. It's just that this is the next thing you can do with leftover bananas. Mash 3 or 4 bananas and add them to ⅔ cup soft butter or margarine which has been creamed with ⅔ cups sugar. Beat in 2 eggs. Sift together 2½ cups flour, 1½ teaspoons baking powder, and 1 teaspoon salt; add this to the banana mixture alternately with ⅔ cup sour cream which has been mixed with 1½ teaspoons baking soda. Beat until well mixed, 2 minutes at medium speed, and pour the batter into 2 buttered 9-inch layer cake pans. Bake the layers 30 to 35 minutes in a 350° F. oven. Cool for 10 minutes before removing from the pans, and cool some more before frosting. I like to stick the layers of a banana cake together with peanut butter mixed with enough soft butter so that the consistency of it won't rip the cake in the spreading. Then I frost the cake with a vanilla frosting. Num.

Coconut is a fruit in which I took a crash course once when I gave a Hawaiian birthday party. Ever since, I can take it or leave it, mostly leave it. Recently though, I needed unsweetened coconut for a recipe and discovered another little-known fact (at least, it was little-, not to say un-known to me) about coconut. All the dry stuff you buy in packages has been sweetened. My, you learn a lot when you read the small print on packages! So naturally I bought a coconut and grated my own unsweetened coconut. Yes, I have an electric coconut grater. It's called a food processor. The recipe called for half a cup of unsweetened coconut and there I was again, stuck with all that coconut. That's what leftovers are all about, isn't it? So I peeled 3 or 4 oranges and sliced them prettily and tossed in a generous handful (about a cup) of freshly grated coconut and laced the whole thing with liquid honey which I poured from the jar, and served it for dessert one night. Gorgeous! Only my kids couldn't stand it. So I gave it to my cleaning lady. Her kids didn't like it, either. But she did. You can decide what you want to do about it. I prefer not to think about it again.

Coconut Bars

Made with my Homemade Biscuit Mix (see page 82), coconut bars are quick and good. Measure 2 cups mix into a mixing bowl and add 1½ cups brown sugar, firmly packed, and 1 cup grated coconut, fresh or packaged. Blend these ingredients with a fork, then stir in ¼ cup oil, 2 eggs, beaten, and 1 teaspoon vanilla. Fold in 1 cup chocolate chips. This is a stiff batter, so don't wrench your hand forcing it into a buttered 13"×9" pan. Bake 25 to 30 minutes in a 350° F. oven.

Biscuit mix
Brown sugar
Coconut
Oil
Eggs
Vanilla
Chocolate chips

Coconut-Pecan Frosting

This frosting is good on Orange Cake (see page 110). Mix together in a small bowl 3 tablespoons butter, melted, 2 tablespoons cream, 5 tablespoons brown sugar, and ½ cup each grated coconut and chopped pecans. Spread on hot-from-the-oven 9-inch cake and bake 10 more minutes at 350° F.

Butter
Cream
Brown sugar
Coconut
Chopped pecans

You'll never find me coping with leftover cranberries because I don't like cranberries. Another thing I don't like is candied rind, so you won't find any recipes here for ways to candy lemon, orange, or grapefruit rind. The magazines are full of that sort of thing at Christmas-time and they can have it. Candied rind may be a great thing to do with leftover rind, but what do you do with leftover *candied* rind? As a matter of fact, I need all the fresh rind I can get because I have a zester and it does such a good job that it's no trick to add grated lemon and orange rind to all kinds of things. Most of the lemons and oranges in my fridge are bald. Consider for a moment what grated lemon or orange rind can do for one's muffins, biscuits, cookies, frostings, quick breads, pie crusts, cream cheese sandwich fillings, date fillings for cookies or date bars, lamb chops, pork chops, veal (wiener schnitzel without lemon? unthinkable!).

Mary Lou's Lemon Bread

Salad oil
Eggs
Milk
Sugar
Lemons
Flour
Baking powder
Baking soda
Salt

Drop into the blender container or food processor bowl (steel blade) 6 tablespoons salad oil, 2 eggs, ½ cup milk, 1 cup sugar, and 1 or 2 whole lemons, quartered. Blend well, then pour the mixture into a big bowl into which you have already sifted 1½ cups flour, 1 teaspoon baking powder, ½ teaspoon baking soda, and ¼ teaspoon salt. Stir well and pour into a buttered 9″ × 5″ × 3″ loaf pan. Bake 1 hour at 350° F. Orange Bread is almost the same as Lemon Bread, but uses the guts of 1 or 2 oranges. A quick bread like this is great for a church party or a spate of new neighbours. Have a coffee party. You never know how many friends you can make with Lemon Bread or Lemon Muffins.

Lemon Muffins

Flour
Baking powder
Salt
Sugar
Lemon rind
Eggs
Corn oil
Lemon juice

Sift together 1 cup flour, 1 teaspoon baking powder, ¼ teaspoon salt, and ½ cup sugar into a bowl; add the grated rind of a lemon if you can find one with its skin intact. Beat 2 eggs, then stir in ½ cup corn oil and ¼ cup lemon juice; lightly stir this mixture into the dry ingredients until they've all been introduced – but just barely. Drop the batter by spoonfuls into buttered muffin pans; bake for 15 minutes in a 400° F. oven. Makes 6 large (3½-inch diameter) or 12 small muffins.

Orange Cake

Corn oil
Brown sugar
Egg
Orange rind and juice
Sour cream or buttermilk
Baking soda
Flour
Baking powder

This is a simple and fast cake for a quick dessert; it removes 2 oranges from your care and refrigeration. Mix ½ cup corn oil, 1 cup brown sugar, firmly packed, 1 egg, and the grated rind and juice of 2 oranges. Stir in ½ cup sour cream or buttermilk mixed with 1 teaspoon baking soda. Sift in 1½ cups flour and 1 teaspoon baking powder. Beat 2 minutes at medium speed; scrape the batter into a buttered 8-inch square pan. Bake 45 to 55 minutes at 350° F. or until done. This is the cake that takes the Coconut-Pecan Frosting (page 109).

But speaking of frosting, Orange Frosting is good on a white cake:

Orange Frosting

In the small bowl of the mixer put the juice and grated rind of 1 orange, 2 tablespoons butter, 2 tablespoons cream, and 1 egg. Beat in 1½ to 2 cups sifted icing sugar – or more – until the frosting is the consistency you want. If you have more frosting than you need, refrigerate the rest.

Orange juice and rind
Butter
Cream
Egg
Icing sugar

By now you may think you have too many little containers of frosting – maybe lemon (you can duplicate the above recipe with the juice and rind of a lemon), chocolate, banana, etc. Don't be afraid to mix them. Lemon and chocolate go well together; so do orange and chocolate. And lemon-orange is beautiful.

Lemon Ice Cream

Beat together 2 cups evaporated milk and 1 cup sugar. Freeze in a flat dish till mushy. Scrape into the mixer bowl and add the grated rinds and juice of 2 lemons; beat again. Freeze for 2 hours. Beat again and then freeze until it's ice cream. For a company dessert, take as many lemons as you have consumers and cut the tops off them, about one quarter of the way down. Cut a little nip off the bottom of each lemon so it will sit flat. Now, with your curved grapefruit knife or whatever instrument strikes you as being effective, scrape the lemon meat out of the lemon, leaving the shell intact. Pack the hollowed-out lemons with lemon ice cream, mounding it up well above the top of the lemon. Return to the freezer on a baking sheet until serving time. That recipe for ice cream will serve eight people, with a possibility of seconds.

Evaporated milk
Sugar
Lemon juice and rind

Use leftover lemon innards, without the rind, in Mary Lou's Lemon Bread (page 110).

The tangible expression of your love for your family is the good dinner you set before them every night. Mind you, some nights they could accuse you of loving them less than other nights, but that is purely an aesthetic judgement. Ethically, you're doing the right thing all the time. It's a constant unending inexorable challenge, this business of coming up with three meals a day, every day. And what's for dessert? If it weren't for fruit, half the time I wouldn't know. Give me one apple, one orange, a banana, and a handful of marshmallows, and I'll give you a dessert with no leftovers.

111

Chapter 8

Bread: Feed the Swans

They aren't royal, of course, but Stratford, Ontario, does have swans on the lake in the summer – the ducks stay all winter, too, paddling the water like mad at times to keep it from freezing; all of them like stale bread. That's a last resort. I don't expect you to go all the way to Stratford to get rid of your bread crusts.

Let's start by filling a few stray hamburger buns with something other than hamburger before they go hard.

Treasure Tuna Buns

Tuna
Hard-boiled eggs
Green onions
Celery
Dill pickle
Cheddar cheese
Mayonnaise
Salt and pepper
Poultry seasoning
Hamburger buns

In a bowl break up with a fork the contents of 1 can tuna, drained. Cut in 2 hard-boiled eggs, 4 green onions, snipped, ½ cup chopped celery, and 1 dill pickle, chopped. Grate about ½ cup Cheddar cheese into the mixture and add enough mayonnaise to bind the whole thing together in a cohesive relationship – start with 2 generous tablespoons and assess it after a few minutes. Add salt and pepper to taste and ½ teaspoon poultry seasoning (this is the secret ingredient) and toss the mixture gently but thoroughly with a fork. Butter 4 or 5 hamburger buns, the number depending on how many you have to use up, and spread the mixture generously, or not so, on each bun. Isn't that one of the hardest things to do in cooking? Making a spread come out even? If you start too big-handed, you end up skimpy; if you're too stingy at the outset you end up with masses of filling oozing all over the kitchen counter. What you need at all times is a steady hand and an appraising eye. Put the lid on each bun and wrap each one separately in a piece of

112

aluminum foil (this is a good way to use up used pieces of foil, too). To serve for lunch, pop them in a 350° F. oven for half an hour or so until the cheese is nice and melty inside. The buns may be refrigerated until you need them; add 10 minutes to the heating time if they're cold. Of course, you can fill leftover hot dog buns with this mixture, too.

Treasure Buns

You can do it with hamburger, too, but you'll need more buns. I often make these with fresh buns for birthday parties because they're so easy to serve and no one gets a chance to start a mustard-squirting contest. You can make a bunch of them ahead of time and freeze them for use when you need them. They're also handy if you have people on staggered meal hours for whatever reason: cub meeting, swimming lesson, work schedule. One or two of these plus a salad equals a fast dinner. One pound of hamburger will service 8 buns. Sauté 2 onions, chopped, in 1 tablespoon oil until they are soft. Add 1 pound ground beef and brown it quickly, breaking it up with a wooden spoon. Stir in 1 teaspoon garlic salt (more if you like it), 1 teaspoon oregano, ½ teaspoon Worcestershire sauce, and a 10-ounce can tomato paste. Cook for a minute or two – just enough to allow an encounter. Butter the bun halves and ladle the filling on the bottom halves with a slotted spoon. Top the filling on each half with a cheese slice to fit, and then put on the lid of the bun. Wrap securely in foil and refrigerate or freeze. To serve, heat in a 350° F. oven for 30 minutes if they have been refrigerated, or 1 hour at 375° F. if they go directly from freezer to oven. You can double or triple this recipe quite easily, the only real limitation (for assembly purposes) being the length of your kitchen counter. Once I made 196 of them for a theatre party, but I had two helpers that day and a very long counter.

Onions
Oil
Ground beef
Garlic salt
Oregano
Worcestershire sauce
Tomato sauce
Buttered hamburger
 buns
Cheese slices

If you come out uneven on the filling, that is, if you run out of buns before you run out of filling, don't panic! You have just acquired one of the most instant casseroles ever. Say you have about 2 cups of filling left, or less. Look in your fridge or your kitchen shelves and add to the stuff in the frying pan some mixed vegetables or canned corn, ½ to 1 cup cooked rice or macaroni, and ½ cup grated Cheddar cheese. Or open a can of kidney beans and dump them in, along with 1 teaspoon chili powder, and pretend you knew what you were doing all along. Result: one fast fast fast luncheon dish, ready after half an hour in a 350° F. oven.

Bill's Corned Beef Slush

Corned beef
Oil or butter
Ketchup
Mustard
Worcestershire sauce
Basil
Salt and pepper
Cheddar cheese
Buttered hamburger
  buns (toasted)

Cut up a 12-ounce can corned beef into a frying pan lubricated with 2 tablespoons oil, butter, or margarine – just enough to get things started. Stir in 4 tablespoons ketchup, 2 tablespoons prepared mustard, 1 tablespoon Worcestershire sauce, and ½ teaspoon crushed basil. Salt and pepper to taste. Cook and stir over medium heat until the corned beef gets nice and oozy, then stir in ½ cup grated Cheddar cheese and keep cooking until the cheese melts. Butter toasted hamburger bun halves and glop the corned beef slush onto them; top each with a cheese slice and pop under the broiler until the cheese has melted. Three buns serve six, but if you have 4 buns, the two adults get 2 halves apiece. Unless one of the kids is bigger than one of the adults.

You can do all the treasure bun and sloshy ideas above with hot dog buns. Our taste buds and associations being what they are, wieners are sort of married to buns. If you have leftover wiener buns you probably have a few leftover wieners, too.

Wieners and Buns

Wieners
Chili sauce
Tomato soup, juice, or
  sauce
Hot dog relish
Mustard
Cheese spread or
  Cheddar cheese
Wiener buns

Cut up from 3 to 6 wieners, and heat them in ½ cup chili sauce mixed with ½ cup undiluted tomato soup (or tomato juice or a 6-ounce can tomato sauce) and ¼ cup hot dog relish. Stir in 1 tablespoon prepared mustard and 1 tablespoon cheese spread or ¼ cup grated Cheddar cheese. Cook and stir until the cheese has melted and the wieners are hot. Spoon over split and toasted wiener buns. This is the gloppy way to do it. If you mince the wieners and omit the tomato soup/juice/sauce, simply mixing the meat with the seasoning things, you can spoon this mixture on buttered buns, wrap them in foil, and heat them in the oven. Why go to all this trouble, you say, when you could just simply serve hot dogs again? Because the number of buns doesn't match the number of wieners, that's why. Have you ever tried to persuade one of your children to eat a hot dog in *a slice of bread*?

On the other hand, there are times when you run out of weiners, before you run out of buns. That's my fault, because I never eat the bun. French-toasted weiner buns are fun with sausages, but you can't pick them up. A bun in the hand is worth two in the breadbox; it gets used up that way.

Fish Dogs

Heat a package of frozen fish sticks according to the directions. Toast and butter and spread with tartar sauce 4 wiener buns. Put 2 fish sticks in each bun (there are usually 8 in a package), and serve to four surprised kids for lunch or a light supper.

Fish sticks
Buttered wiener buns
 (toasted)
Tartar sauce

Banana Dogs

I invented this one long before I ever saw it in a magazine, but I guess it's something lots of people must have thought of. Simply spread hot dog buns, plain or toasted, depending on how stale they are, with butter and peanut butter and put a whole peeled banana in each one. Even nicer, they tell me, with chunky peanut butter.

Hot dog buns
Butter
Peanut butter
Banana(s)

Peanut Butter or Cheese and Bacon Broils

Broil 8 slices bacon until almost cooked; drain on paper toweling. Toast 4 split wiener buns under the broiler. Butter them, spread them with peanut butter, and put a slice of bacon on each half. Broil until the bacon is crisp and the peanut butter melty. You can do the same with cheese spread and bacon.

Bacon
Buttered wiener buns
Peanut butter or cheese
 spread

Sausage Dogs

I learned this one from the market in Kitchener, Ontario. Fry a good country sausage, cut in lengths to fit the buns, until it is cooked; place it in a warmed, mustarded wiener bun along with a generous heaping of hot sauerkraut. The wet sauerkraut softens the bun.

Country sausage
Mustard
Wiener buns
Sauerkraut

Leftover rye bread makes good chapons. It makes good croutons, too, but you can't keep croutons on the shelf. I hate to be pedantic about this, but what are called croutons in the store and sell at outrageous prices are really chapons. Croutons are cubes of bread that have been toasted in butter or oil. Obviously they will not keep, but will go rancid. Chapons are dry-toasted, and keep indefinitely in a tightly closed canister. So I cut whatever is left of a loaf of rye bread into small cubes, spread them out in a roasting pan, sprinkle them heavily with garlic salt, and leave them in a 250° F. oven for hours. Every once in a while I muddle them around with my hands to get all the surfaces exposed to the heat. When they are nice and crisp and golden brown (the time varies according to the staleness of the bread I started with), I let them cool before storing in a closed canister. Very handy to have on hand for Caesar salad and French onion soup.

Rye bread (or French bread) is good toasted and spread with garlic butter, eaten alone, or used as a base for sliced steak or cold cuts. Even 5 or 6 slices of rye or French bread can be buttered with your ever-present store of garlic butter, wrapped in foil, heated, and served as a fast accompaniment for plates of spaghetti or whatever. Rye bread, toasted, can also serve as the base for Corned Beef Slush if you have no hamburger buns.

If you overestimate the amount of pancake batter people are going to use, there are two things you can do about it. You can store the uncooked batter in the fridge and within the next day or so cook pancakes again, adding 1 teaspoon baking bowder and a little milk to the batter to liven it up and thin it. Or you can go ahead and cook all the pancakes at once and then cope with them at your leisure. They freeze well in plastic bags. For a quick breakfast later on, they can be popped into the toaster and served with brown sugar or syrup.

Freeze leftover waffles just as you freeze pancakes, and heat them in the toaster to serve. Using waffles as a foundation for creamed things is a long-accepted idea. Practically nothing fights with a waffle. Creamed vegetables, creamed chicken or ham, whatever. Recently I had a little leftover oyster stew (with no oysters). I thickened the milky mixture and sliced 2 hard-boiled eggs into it to heat. Spooned over a waffle, it made lunch for one. If you're stuck for dessert, serve 2 frozen waffle sections (toaster-heated) with ice cream between them. Do ice cream sandwiches ever go out of style?

Bread crumbs of any kind are endlessly useful. You can mix them with grated cheese or not, as you prefer, sprinkle them over almost any casserole, and dot them with butter. They always make the casserole look as if you *cared*. They make an excellent binder for meat loaves and salmon loaves, liver patties, Swedish meatballs, and gefilte fish. They also serve as a base for dipping fish fillets, veal steaks, chicken pieces, etc., for frying purposes.

116

But sometimes bread crumbs as such begin to pall, and you have to cope with larger amounts of superannuated bread than you care to. Keep a Pudding and/or a Stuffing Bag in the freezer, just as you keep a Soup Bag. For the Pudding Bag, save the last lone hardy muffin that everyone ignored, the antiquated doughnut, the kernel-hard corn stick, the rocklike cinnamon bun, the wiener bun that all your ingenuity and wit could not save from petrification. Things like that. Best tear them up a bit before you freeze them; they're easier to handle that way. Then when you have a bagful you can make a bread pudding.

Into your Stuffing Bag you put breads that are more amenable to a salty ending: a heel of French or rye bread that wasn't worth making into chapons, a withered onion bun, a Parker House roll beyond recall. And of course, heels and crusts of ordinary bread too far gone for sandwiches or toast. The variety adds to the flavour of your stuffing. Again, tear up the bread before you freeze it. If you have more stuffing than you need for the average bird, it will freeze in a plastic bag and next time you have almost-instant stuffing (allow for thawing time) for your chicken or turkey.

Toast Cups

If you want cup shapes, press stale bread slices (crusts removed) into muffin cups and brush them with melted butter. Toast or broil in the oven (350° F. or 4 to 6 inches from the broiler) until they are golden. Big croutons are inch-thick slices, crusts removed, buttered and toasted till golden – delightful under Cornish game hens or a definitive piece of chicken per person.

Stale bread slices
Melted butter

Poppy Seed Toast

Butter stale bread slices and broil them just until the butter starts to sizzle. Sprinkle the slices generously, that is, solidly, with crushed poppy seeds and toast some more. Cut into fingers and serve hot – nice instead of biscuits for dinner. But if you were to spread the toast with honey before you sprinkled on the poppy seeds, you'd have a lovely nibble with afternoon tea. Stack the slices together and keep them warm in foil until ready to serve.

Stale bread slices
Butter
Poppy seeds

Garlic Toast

Butter
Garlic
Stale bread slices

Put a large dollop of butter or margarine in a small saucepan and with a garlic press crush into it 4 or 5 cloves garlic. Melt the butter and stir in the garlic, but don't let the butter separate. Toast slices of stale bread under the broiler and then brush with the garlic butter; serve immediately. Tuck it between folds of aluminum foil so it will stay hot but not ruin a napkin with butter.

Sweet breads seem to disappear faster than plain breads, but even they can linger on and outlive their popularity. If you ever have stale raisin bread, wrap it in foil and bake.

Raisin Cardamom Toast

Butter
Sugar
Cardamom
Stale raisin bread slices

Mash ½ cup soft butter (or however much you think you need for the amount of bread you are dealing with) with 3 tablespoons sugar and 1 teaspoon ground cardamom. Spread it on slices of stale raisin bread, put the slices together to form whatever part of the loaf is left, wrap the whole thing in foil, and warm for 20 to 25 minutes in a 325° F. oven. Never underestimate the power of aluminum foil.

I don't buy the proverb that says half a loaf is better than none. I prefer the attitude of the American humorist Josh Billings, who said, "If you can't get a half a loaf take a whole one – a whole loaf is better than no bread." But a whole loaf can go stale faster than half a loaf because it takes longer to use it up. If you're really worried about having stale bread in your bread box, there is one foolproof solution I haven't mentioned. Bake your own bread.

Chapter 9

Odds and Ends: Situational Ethics for Extraneous Miscellanies

I think that the graduate school of cookery must be affiliated with the School of Life that my father was always telling me about when I was a child. You never get a diploma; there's a test every day; the course is intensive and prolonged; you're always learning something new. Too many graduate cooks take their skill and experience for granted. It's difficult not to. Where once I needed to know *exactly* how much of what to put in a recipe, I now have the confidence to trust that if you are patient with food, and love it, and bring it along, it will reward you by being tractable and edible. Patience cannot be measured. Neither can leftovers. All the graduate cook can do is keep her wits about her. She must cope swiftly with whatever situation (read leftover) presents itself, and in whatever context comes to hand. Then she carries on as did the man who explained to the judge how he came to throw the brick through the window: "It seemed the appropriate thing to do at the time."

Take wine. I do. So did my husband. And our guests. Although I must admit that my consumption of wine seems to have crept up over the years, still there *are* times when we do not finish a bottle. Certainly everyone has discovered that it is perfectly possible to put the remains of a bottle of wine in the fridge and to serve it the next day. The bouquet may not suit the connoisseur, of course, but it's still quite palatable. And if there's not enough for two of you? Rejoice. A heel of wine, now and then, is all you need to guarantee your never having to buy another bottle of wine vinegar. All you need do to keep your own supply constant is keep adding wine heels to your wine vinegar bottle, making sure there is enough vinegar in the bottom of the bottle to act as a culture and thus start your wine on its way to vinaigrette immortality. Red or white – just keep two separate bottles.

When your vinegar bottles are full, you can turn the wine's attention to other recurring problems. Sauces, stews, soups, casseroles – all can profit by the judicious addition of an appropriate quarter or half cup of wine. A little extra wine in a marinade never did any meat anything but good and it raises an *au jus* pan sauce to gourmet levels.

The first time I ever had a really large party I borrowed one of those enormous 60-cup coffee makers from my friendly neighbourhood supermarket and ended up with about 50 cups left over. That turned out to be one party where it seemed no one felt like drinking coffee. I minimized my subsequent problems with leftover coffee with the help of my mother and my husband. My mother gave me a 30-cup coffee maker, which lowers the odds on leftover coffee. My husband got to the coffee maker first and poured out the leftover coffee before my Puritan conscience had a chance to assess it and feel guilty about it. However, I still remember my first attempts to cope with large amounts of leftover coffee and it's only fair that I pass on what I learned. The main thing that's wrong with most recipes calling for coffee is that they call too softly. What's 1 tablespoon here or there to a girl who's holding 3 gallons? What you're looking for is not a mild mocha flavour in what you're cooking, but *Real Coffee*.

Coffee Jelly

Gelatin
Coffee
Coffee liqueur
Cognac
Sugar

Soften 1 tablespoon unflavoured gelatin in ¼ cup cold coffee. Heat together 1½ cups coffee with ¼ cup coffee liqueur, 2 tablespoons cognac, and ¼ cup sugar. Stir in the gelatin, pour the liquid into a pretty 2-cup mould, and chill until set. Serve with lots of whipped cream. It's sort of a still-life Spanish Coffee. Serves four.

My Swedish part-time cook taught me this best of all gravies to accompany a lamb roast.

Coffee Gravy

Measure (with your eye, if it's accurate enough) the drippings in the roasting pan and match the amount with flour. Working on a ratio of 2 tablespoons drippings to 2 tablespoons flour – which you have sprinkled over the pan and stirred briskly with a wooden spoon to prevent lumping as it cooks over medium-high heat – add 1 cup coffee with cream and sugar in it. Stir this in diligently until you have a smooth and probably too-thick gravy. Add enough stock to thin the gravy to your desired consistency, add salt and pepper to taste, and pour into a preheated gravy boat. Preheat your gravy boat with boiling water and give the last person served a fighting chance for hot gravy.

Meat drippings
Flour
Coffee with cream and sugar
Stock
Salt and pepper

There are some gallons to go.

Coffee Muffins

Sift 2 cups flour with 4 teaspoons baking powder, ½ cup sugar, and ½ teaspoon salt. Beat 1 egg; combine with 1⅓ cups cold coffee and 2 tablespoons corn oil. Stir all at once into the dry ingredients and don't overdo the stirring, for the muffins' sake. Spoon the batter into greased muffin pans and bake in a 400° F. oven for 20 to 25 minutes. Makes about 18 muffins. An optional ingredient is ½ cup chopped pecans. Optional means, if you can afford pecans.

Flour
Baking powder
Sugar
Salt
Egg
Coffee
Corn oil
Pecans (optional)

Here is what I love:

Coffee Ice Cream

Stir together 4 cups evaporated milk, 1 cup coffee, ⅛ teaspoon salt, 1 teaspoon vanilla, and 1 cup sugar. Pour into a 13″×9″ pan and freeze until mushy. Remove from freezer, pour into mixing bowl, and beat like mad on high speed. Return to freezer, freeze 2 hours, beat like mad again, then freeze till solid.

Evaporated milk
Coffee
Salt
Vanilla
Sugar

You can serve the rest of your coffee iced, having had the foresight to freeze several ice-cube trays of coffee. Fill glasses with coffee ice cubes and into each glass place 1 teaspoon lemon juice and 2 teaspoons sugar, or to taste. Fill with cold coffee, stir, and serve. You can do the same with iced tea, using fresh hot double-strength tea, suitably lemoned and sugared, poured over frozen tea cubes. More people should freeze cubes of other than water.

I have read that cold tea is good for watering plants, but I'm no gardener, indoor or out, so I never put this theory to the test. I remember an old saying that some women are born to wield a trowel, some a spoon, some a needle, and some a duster. Very male chauvinist saying, that. Anyway, I guess I'm the spoon type myself.

I guess it's my bad arithmetic, but I never seem to come out even on my glacéed fruits and stuff at Christmas baking time. I bake a lot, and I try to figure out exactly how much citron, cherries, pineapple, nuts, raisins, etc., I will need, and I always end up a) buying more, and b) having some left over. You can't leave them on your cupboard shelf for too long, for no matter how you store them, they seem to ooze and get sticky or crystallize. Nuts, of course, go rancid on the shelf. You can always freeze them, safely bagged in plastic, but sooner or later you will have to use them. I look forward to my surplus every year because this has become a standard leftover-based goody.

Fruit Bars

Eggs
Icing sugar
Melted butter
Flour
Baking powder
Salt
Nuts
Dates
Glacéed fruits

Beat 3 eggs with a rotary beater till foamy and then beat in 1¼ cups sifted icing sugar. Stir in 2 tablespoons melted butter or margarine. Sift together 1 cup flour, 1½ teaspoons baking powder, and 1 teaspoon salt; stir into the egg-sugar mixture. Now stir in 3 cups chopped nuts, cut-up dates, and cut-up glacéed fruits – in any proportions your cupboard shelf dictates. If you're short of 3 cups, make up the difference with raisins. Mix well with a wooden spoon and pack into a buttered 9-inch square pan. Bake in a preheated 350° F. oven for 35 to 40 minutes. Cool on a rack and cut in squares to store – they don't last long in a hungry family.

For the next recipe you need not use the glacéed fruits intended for baking. Often at Christmas you receive one of those attractive basket trays of large glacéed fruits, outrageously sweet and meant for indolent nibbling. No one in our house ever touches one after

122

Christmas Day. Use your blender and make a beautiful fruit bread. In this case, the blender is preferable to the food processor because unless you watch the f.p. like a hawk, you're liable to end up with a pink mush.

Post-Christmas Fruit Bread

Sift into a bowl 2¼ cups flour, 2 teaspoons baking powder, ½ teaspoon nutmeg, and ½ teaspoon salt. Into your faithful blender drop ¼ cup corn oil, 1 cup milk, 2 eggs, 1 teaspoon vanilla, and 1 cup sugar. Blend briefly; add 2 cups of a combination of glacéed fruits, currants or raisins, and nuts. If the glacéed fruits are very large, cut them up a bit beforehand to help the blender with its work. Blend until well and truly mixed but lumpy, about 20 seconds; pour the wet into the dry ingredients. Stir to mix well, then pour the batter into a buttered 9× 5× 3″ loaf pan. Bake 50 to 60 minutes in a 350° F. oven. If you don't have the big glacéed fruits, of course, use the packaged pieces. If you don't have enough of everything mentioned above to make 2 cups, make up the difference with coconut. The bread will still be good; it simply varies from time to time depending on the proportions of the fruits and nuts you put into it.

Flour
Baking powder
Nutmeg
Salt
Corn oil
Milk
Eggs
Vanilla
Sugar
Glacéed fruits
Currants or raisins

The big glacéed fruits that no one has eaten will also make a very impressive decor for your New Year ham – if you happen to cook a New Year ham. Carve the bigger fruits into decorative shapes and pin them with toothpicks to the skinned, scored, baked ham in a pretty arrangement. Slap on whatever glaze you have in mind and pop the ham back into the oven for half an hour while you prepare all the other things to go with baked ham. The fruit does nice things for the meat, both taste- and appearance-wise.

You can also make a really fruity filling for a quick coffee cake and get rid of more fruits and peel.

There's always someone at every party who eats all the cashews. Then you're left with a bowl full of abandoned and depressed mixed nuts. They're not only left over, they're left out. Pick out the Brazil nuts, if there are any, because they're so hard they'll break the nut chopper blade. You can sliver them with a sharp knife and stir them into the green beans some night, or dip one end of them into melted cooled dipping chocolate, and allow one each to the kids or you'll never get any yourself. Put the rest of the nuts through the nut chopper or give them a whirl with the steel blade of the f.p. and measure out a cup of them.

Nut Bar Cookies

Butter
Sugar
Flour
Eggs
Brown sugar
Vanilla
Melted butter
Baking powder
Salt
Nuts

Mix together ½ cup butter or margarine, ¼ cup sugar, and 1 cup flour – might as well use the mixer (small bowl) – and pack into a 9-inch square pan. Bake 15 minutes in a preheated 350° F. oven. Meanwhile, drop into the used bowl 2 eggs, beaten, with 1½ cups brown sugar, packed, 1 teaspoon vanilla, 1½ tablespoons melted butter or margarine, 3 tablespoons flour, 1 teaspoon baking powder, and ½ teaspoon salt. Beat for 1 or 2 minutes, until well blended, then stir in 1 cup chopped nuts, your choice: pecans, if you're feeling rich, walnuts, or – and this is why this recipe is here – any mixed combination of leftover nuts you have. If you use salted nuts, omit the salt in the recipe. Spread this mixture on top of the semi-baked stuff in the pan and return it to the oven for another 20 to 30 minutes. You can also use the last of your raisins and currants instead of nuts in this. Store covered with foil – preferably in the fridge, because this mixture is runny.

Here is a way to use up all your Christmas baking nuts; it's so good you might deliberately allow for it.

Spiced Nuts

Sugar
Cardamom
Nutmeg
Evaporated milk
Water
Mixed nuts

Mix together in a saucepan 1 cup sugar, 1 teaspoon cardamom, and ⅛ teaspoon nutmeg. Add ½ cup evaporated milk and 1 tablespoon water and boil to the soft ball stage, 236° F., on a candy thermometer, stirring all the while. Patience. Remove from the heat and quickly stir in 3 cups mixed nuts: pecans, walnuts, almonds, Brazils, etc., but NO peanuts! Keep the nuts as unbroken as possible. Stir till the spoon stops, then turn out on waxed paper or foil to cool. Separate the nuts with your fingers when they're cool enough to handle and allow them to dry. These are nice hostess gifts. Pack them in a thick brandy snifter, the kind you keep getting flowers in, and seal the top with plastic wrap.

Almonds are seldom a problem because they're so versatile. Plain, toasted, slivered, or ground, they can find their way into lots of

124

good things to eat. Slivered and toasted, of course, they can be tossed with green beans and butter and abandon for a company vegetable. Or with Brussels sprouts (you'd serve Brussels sprouts to *company?*). They can mix into breads or on top of. Try chopped almonds, say ½ cup, mixed with 2 tablespoons sugar and ½ teaspoon ground cardomon or cinnamon, sprinkled on a coffee cake before baking, or a pudding before chilling. Nice on Mary Lou's Lemon Bread, too (see page 110). Split in half, almonds make decorations for cookies or yeast breads; ground, they're delicious in cookies. There are cookies called Snickerdoodles which end up being rolled in sugar and cinnamon just before going into the oven. Try rolling a cookie like that in sugar mixed with ground almonds for a change. Toasted and chopped, almonds coat the outside of a cheese log (see Cheese Log). Chopped or un-, they're a lovely crunchy addition to a chicken salad. Rather than let a handful of almonds left over from your Christmas cake recipe go rancid, chop them and mix them with garlic or chili salt, to sprinkle on casseroles. They won't go rancid because they won't be around that long.

Peanuts have such a distinctive flavour they sort of overpower other things. If you have leftover peanuts, small amounts, chop them up and add them to dry cereal for those ubiquitous marshmallow squares every kid knows how to make. Or sprinkle them on top of chicken soup. Or toss them in butter with fresh cooked Brussels sprouts, if you still eat Brussels sprouts. If you have more peanuts to cope with than that, make Peanut Brittle.

The Easiest Peanut Brittle You Ever Heard Of

Put 1 cup sugar and ¾ teaspoon salt in a heavy saucepan and heat and stir it with a wooden spoon over medium-high heat, stirring constantly, until the sugar melts and caramelizes. Quickly stir in ½ to 1 cup peanuts, then pour the stuff into a buttered foil pie pan before it hardens in the saucepan. That's all. Break it up when it's cool.

Sugar
Salt
Peanuts

Don't forget the food processor makes the best peanut butter in the whole world: no sugar, no hydrogenated oil, no additives. But if you want slow nibbling instead of fast spreading try this.

Chili Nuts

Oil
Mustard seed
Chili powder
Garlic salt
Unsalted peanuts

Heat 2 tablespoons oil in a large heavy frying pan over medium-high heat. Stir in 1 tablespoon mustard seed and heat and stir until the seeds pop. Remove from heat; stir in 1¼ tablespoons chili powder and 2 teaspoons garlic salt. Stir in 2 cups unsalted peanuts and toss. Heat over low heat, tossing occasionally, until the nuts are coated and permeated with the chili seasoning. If you have salted peanuts to use up, omit the garlic salt.

Jams and jellies and syrups can be left over, too; sometimes they present not only a sticky problem but also a container problem. You simply run out of preserve pots and pitchers to serve them in and you have to consolidate or move. Don't expect your kids to help you; they will not eat winy grape jelly or sugary jam of any kind, and if the syrup is sluggish they haven't the patience to wait for it.

This is no time to be a purist. Although the accepted glaze for a fruit tart is currant, it is perfectly possible to melt almost any jelly you have an overabundance of crystallizing in your cupboard and pour it over the strawberries or raspberries in a pie shell – it will look and taste fine. You can take almost any jelly, too, and melt it with some ground cloves and dry mustard, then pour it over a baked ham as a quickie glaze. Sugary jams and jellies will not be ignored if you spoon them into large diamonds of the last of your pastry, turn the pastry over on itself, bake it in the oven along with the pie you just made, and let the kids eat the turnovers you just happen to be thoughtful enough to have made. And nobody is going to refuse to eat an ice cream sundae with a dollop of jam or jelly or syrup on top of it. The Post-Christmas Coffee Cake can easily take up to a cup of jam or jelly spread over its surface instead of the fruit topping. Perhaps you should add a teaspoon of cinnamon to the jelly before you spread it on the batter.

Marmalade is something I am always using up. John likes it; no one else does. He eats it with enthusiasm for a week or so and then neglects it. No matter. Mixed with 1 teaspoon cloves, 1 cup marmalade makes a really effective ham glaze and has enough lumps in it that no other decorating is necessary. And my Auntie Anna, of the fish recipe and bran bread Annas, has a good way to use up the marmalade.

126

Marmalade Bread

Into your cooperative neighbourhood blender or food processor bowl (steel blade) drop ½ to 1 cup marmalade, depending on how much you have to use up, 3 tablespoons corn oil, ¾ cup sugar, 1 egg, and ¾ cup milk. Blend till smooth. Into a bowl sift 2½ cups flour, ½ teaspoon salt, 4 teaspoons baking powder. Mix the wet stuff into the dry stuff, slap it into a buttered 9″ × 5″ × 3″ loaf pan, and bake for 1 hour and 15 minutes in a preheated 350° F. oven.

Marmalade
Corn oil
Sugar
Egg
Milk
Flour
Salt
Baking powder

Syrups, too, do hang on and get more and more glicky as time passes. If in the spring I have syrup left over from my previous year's stock, I use it up on two gorgeous desserts.

Maple Slurp Pie

In a large bowl beat 4 egg yolks into 2 cups maple syrup. In the top of a double boiler stir 2 tablespoons cornstarch with 1 cup milk until the cornstarch is dissolved. Add ⅛ teaspoon salt and the egg-syrup mixture. Cook and stir over boiling water until the mixture thickens. Remove from the heat, stir in 1 tablespoon butter, and allow to cool. Pour the filling into a baked 8-inch pie shell and top with meringue: beat 3 egg whites till stiff, then beat in 2 tablespoons sugar. Pile on the pie, sealing the edges, and bake 5 to 8 minutes in a 400° F. oven. Slurp.

Eggs, separated
Maple syrup
Cornstarch
Milk
Salt
Butter
Pie shell
Sugar

Maple Syrup Cake

Combine 1 cup maple syrup and ½ cup milk and save it. Sift together 2½ cups flour, ½ cup sugar, 3 teaspoons baking powder, 1 teaspoon salt. Now add ½ cup soft butter or margarine, 1 teaspoon vanilla, and 1 cup of the maple-milk. Beat for 2 minutes on medium speed of the mixer. Add 2 eggs, beaten, and the remaining ½ cup maple-milk and beat an additional 2 minutes. Turn into 2 greased and floured 9-inch layer cake pans and bake 30 to 35 minutes at 350° F. When cool, frost with Faigie's Frosting (see page 71) and drizzle a maple-fudgey syrup on it to look pretty. Syrup: cook ½ cup maple syrup and ¼ cup sugar to the soft ball stage (236° F.). Drizzle on the cake (quickly!) before the syrup hardens.

Maple syrup
Milk
Flour
Sugar
Baking powder
Salt
Butter
Vanilla
Eggs

Now we have reached the no-man's-land of your fridge door shelves and your bottle and jar shelves. It's clean-up time. Just so it won't be too much of a wrench to part with old friends, I'll give you one you won't part with.

Soy Sauce Marinade for Chicken

Soy sauce
Bottled French dressing
Ketchup
Water
Dry mustard
Chicken wings

Mix together 1 cup Japanese soy sauce, an 8-ounce bottle French dressing (or the remains of 2 old bottles of dressing, as long as one of them is French), ½ cup ketchup, ¾ cup water, and 1 teaspoon dry mustard. Pour this over about 3 pounds chicken wings in a shallow pan, cover, and let them marinate at least 3 hours, or overnight, in the fridge. Now when I say 3 pounds, I'm guessing. I always count my chicken wings. I allow at least 6 per person and if we're lucky we get to eat some cold for lunch the next day. Bake the wings, covered, for 40 minutes in a 350° F. oven. Then pour off the sauce but *don't throw it away!* Turn on the broiler now and brown the chicken wings for 20 minutes, turning once or twice and basting with the sauce if necessary. Serve hot, with plenty of paper napkins. Cool the baste/marinade, skim off any fat, and freeze the baste/marinade in a plastic container. It will also keep in the fridge. Next time you want chicken wings, thaw it and use it again. Every once in a while you'll have to add more soy sauce or the heel of a bottle of French dressing, according to your taste and the amount depleted. It is a self-perpetuating marinade and will last a whole winter this way, getting richer and more jelly-like as time passes, so that eventually you will have to melt it in order to pour it on the chicken wings.

Sauces for Fondue Bourguignonne

Garlic butter
Curry dip
Jelly and horseradish
Capers or gherkins and
  mayonnaise
Tartar sauce

Just check your fridge and start improvising. I hope you have a little dish full of garlic butter (see Garlic Butter) somewhere because that's my favourite accompaniment to beef fondue. Also some of that leftover Sour Cream Dip (see page 57) for crudités is very good. If in spite of what I have said about using up jelly, you have jelly, mix it with the heel of a jar of horseradish – sweet-hot is good with meat. Plum sauce and chili sauce mix amazingly well. The last of a jar of capers and ditto of a jar of gherkins blended into mayonnaise can be pseudo-rémoulade sauce. If you have a heel of tartar sauce, add that, too.

128

A Chinese Hot Pot, or what the Japanese call *mizutaki*, is a lower-calorie type of fondue. Your pot is filled with chicken stock (homemade, of course) and your platters are filled with a choice of slender-cut raw vegetables such as mushrooms, asparagus, turnip, Chinese cabbage, and cherry tomatoes. In addition you offer any of the following for the protein part: scallops, cut in half if they are large; lightly poached shrimp; breast of chicken, cut in thin slices and previously marinated in a mixture of soy sauce and ground fresh gingerroot; and flank steak, also thinly sliced (slice it when it's partially frozen), and marinated to your taste. Give everyone a little strainer (easier than chopsticks for handling the food) and let each pack it as he wishes with the food he will cook in the simmering soup. At the end of the cooking and eating process, serve the soup, which has become incredibly good because of all the good things cooked in it. I'm getting to the sauces and the using up of your jars and bottles right now. Soy sauce, of course (there's no such thing as leftover soy sauce), plum sauce, jelly thinned and sharpened with a little vinegar – all these are good condiments with the fish and meat you're cooking. A dollop of cold hollandaise mixed with sour cream would be nice with the asparagus. Hot mustard, freshly made (because homemade hot mustard dries out in the dish if you leave it lying around), is good with the steak. I leave it to you and your fridge.

The question will arise: what happens to the dibs and dabs of sauces left over from the fondue or the hot pot or just plain left over? If you're daring enough, drop everything into the blender, empty almost every bottle and jar in the house, rinsing out the gummy chili sauce, the plum sauce dregs, the horseradish, what have you, from the myriad containers surrounding you. Add a can of tomato soup and an onion, quartered, to make you feel you are contributing something. Blend everything thoroughly. What you have is an incredible sparerib sauce. If anyone asks you for the recipe, smile inscrutably; neither of you could ever repeat it. Put all the glass jars out for the glass recycling pickup and be grateful for your recycled shelves.

Throughout this book I have kept referring to the sloosh from a ketchup bottle. I'm sure everyone knows what I'm talking about, but just in case: you take a ketchup bottle with a recalcitrant sludge in the bottom, pour in about ½ cup very hot water, cap the bottle, and shake it hard to loosen all that tomato goodness. Pour the resulting sloosh into whatever you're cooking. The same applies to mustard and relish jars, chili and barbecue sauce bottles, whatever. For the last of the coleslaw dressing or French dressing – if you buy these things instead of making your own – rinse out the bottle with a little vinegar and add this liquid to your next tossed salad.

There remains only this to consider – what you do with leftovers from The Rich Life. Every once in a while you blow a bundle for a special occasion and buy some special expensive food. What a shame if you cannot find a delectable conclusion for the leftovers, for there will be some. Leftovers are as inevitable as death and taxes. Take caviar, but not too often. There are some quite good North American approximations of genuine Russian beluga caviar which will not break your budget. We'll assume we're talking about this. Just remember what G. K. Chesterton said: "There is more simplicity in the man who eats caviar on impulse than in the man who eats grapenuts on principle." Think about it.

Blinis With Caviar and Sour Cream

Eggs
Brandy
Milk
Water
Oil
Flour
Salt
Baking powder
Icing sugar
Caviar
Sour cream
Tabasco sauce

Make the pancake batter first: into your food processor bowl (steel blade), drop 2 eggs, 1 tablespoon brandy, ⅔ cup milk, ⅓ cup water, and 1 tablespoon oil. Sift together ¾ cup flour, ½ teaspoon salt, 2 teaspoons baking powder, and 1 tablespoon icing sugar; add to mixture in bowl. Blend for 20 seconds, transfer to a pitcher, and let stand in the fridge, covered, for at least 1 hour. When you're ready to cook the pancakes, stir up the batter; pour enough of it into a very hot, lightly oiled small frying pan to cover the bottom. Tilt the pan as you pour the batter in so that the minimum amount of batter will cover the maximum amount of pan. Cook quickly over high heat, turning once. I have done this in my chafing dish in the living room so I don't miss the conversation, and on the griddle on the gas barbecue outside. As each pancake is ready, serve at once, transferring it quickly to a small plate. On the pancake put 1 teaspoon caviar, 1 teaspoon fork-whipped sour cream, and a drop or two of Tabasco sauce. Roll up the pancake with the edge of a fork and serve, untouched by human hands, with a fork and a napkin. Don't try to take care of more than six people with these. Six are willing to wait their turn for helpings; more people than that are liable to get impatient and turn ugly.

An expensive pâté you have bought for a small cocktail or dinner party can serve more than you thought if you treat the leftovers gently. You can spoon little dollops of it into tiny turnovers

130

(made from leftover pastry dough) and bake them for 8 or 10 minutes in the same oven with your pie. You can mash it and stuff it into mushroom caps and get more mileage out of it that way. Or you could shape and slice it into uniform rounds and maybe get enough to put a slice on each of the steaks or hamburgers you are serving to discriminating people. By discriminating, I mean don't try this on the kids. They'll just make nasty comments about ruining a perfectly good hamburger.

Finally, a bouquet of miscellanies. Did you know you can freeze Hallowe'en suckers and distribute them at your discretion throughout the year? They don't stick together in the freezer the way they do on the kitchen shelf. Chocolates and nuts can be frozen: put the nuts in plastic bags and wrap chocolates in their boxes in freezer wrap. Leftover Christmas hard candy can be melted over low heat and used as an ice cream sauce; add a little water if it's too thick. Peppermint candy canes can be hammered in a plastic bag, then stirred into softened vanilla or strawberry or chocolate ice cream which, refrozen solid, becomes peppermint stick ice cream. If Christmas fruitcake becomes a problem, say about July, break it up and stir it into softened ice cream. Refreeze and call it Tutti Frutti Ice Cream when you serve it. I won't tell.

Even if I did, it wouldn't do me any good. You may never do it again. Leftover cooking is top-of-the-head cooking; the key words are *improvise* and *ad lib*. Sufficient unto the day is the solution thereof. Who knows what tomorrow's leftovers may be? Only your fridge will know for sure. Talk to it. Don't tell me your problems, I have enough of my own. Right now there's a container of sauerkraut that's been in my fridge for too long. Seems to me there's an old-fashioned cake recipe using sauerkraut ... I think I'll try it, and see what happens.

Index